BRECHT
As They Knew Him

INTERNATIONAL PUBLISHERS
381 Park Avenue South NEW YORK, N. Y. 10016

Brecht

As They Knew Him

A man who had not seen
Herr K. for a long time greeted
him with the words:
"You haven't changed at all."
"Oh!", said Herr K.,
and paled.

Brecht,
Stories of Herr Keuner

Brecht

As They Knew Him

Hubert Witt
Editor

John Peet
Translator

International
Publishers
New York

Published simultaneously by
International Publishers, New York,
Lawrence & Wishart, London,
and Seven Seas Books, Berlin, 1974

Library of Congress Cataloging in Publication Data
Witt, Hubert, comp.
Brecht — as they knew him.
Translation of Erinnerungen an Brecht.
Bibliography: p.
1. Brecht, Bertolt, 1898–1956.   I. Title.
PT2603.R397Z9613   852'.9'12   (B)   74-8244
ISBN 0-7178-0415-1

Acknowledgments

Seven Seas Books wishes to thank the authors, their publishers and representatives for the right to include in English translation the selections in this volume. To

Verlag Philipp Reclam Jun., Leipzig, for selections by Ruth Berlau, Paul Dessau, Hanns Eisler, Bernard Guillemin, Elisabeth Hauptmann, Wieland Herzfelde, Angelika Hurwicz, Hanns Otto Münsterer, Vladimir Pozner, Bernhard Reich, Käthe Rülicke-Weiler, Ernst Schumacher, Anna Seghers, Erwin Strittmatter, Sergei Tretyakov, Berthold Viertel, Manfred Wekwerth and the Stage Technicians;

Aufbau-Verlag, Berlin und Weimar, for selections by Konstantin Fedin, Herbert Jhering, Günter Kunert, Max Schroeder, Arnold Zweig and the poem by Johannes R. Becher;

Henschelverlag Kunst und Gesellschaft, Berlin, for selections by Caspar Neher, Paul Rilla, and for "Bertolt Brecht the Director";

Verlag Kurt Desch, Munich, for selections by Arnolt Bronnen and Günther Weisenborn;

Werner Mittenzwei for "Brecht 1973 . . .";

Lotte Lenya-Weill for "Threepenny Opera";

Marta Feuchtwanger for "Bertolt Brecht Presented to the British" by Lion Feuchtwanger;

Suhrkamp Verlag, Frankfurt am Main and New Left Books, London (U. K. rights), for "From the Brecht Commentary" by Walter Benjamin.

For the right to include selections from *Diary 1946—1949* by Max Frisch (copyright Suhrkamp Verlag edition) we wish to thank the author, Suhrkamp Verlag, Frankfurt am Main, and Harcourt Brace Jovanovich, New York.

For permission to include the lines from *Stories of Herr Keuner* by Bertolt Brecht we wish to thank Associated Book Publishers, London; Methuen & Co., London and Mr. Kurt Bernheim, New York.

Contents

Editor's Note

Goethe, looking back on his life's work, said: "What am I myself? What have I done? Everything which I have seen, heard and observed I have collected and utilised. My works have been nurtured by uncounted different individuals, by fools and wise men, people of spirit and dullards; childhood, maturity, old age have all given me their thoughts, their abilities, hopes and views; I have often reaped what others have sown. My work is that of a collective being bearing the name Goethe."

Brecht held the opinion that "without outside help, only with the sparse material which an individual can carry in his arms" it was possible to erect a scanty hut, but never great and lasting buildings. He knew how to invite many people to work with him creatively and critically, thanks to the power of his ideas, the attraction of his thought, the conviction in his laughter, the greatness and consistency of his will. All these people brought with them their thoughts, abilities, hopes and views, their experiences and their contradictions — the casual conversational partner as well as the regular collaborator.

Working to change social conditions, and thereby changing himself, Brecht helped his collaborators too to change; and he helped also to change his readers, who derived understanding and impetus from his works, and became in the widest sense his assistants. Some of his assistants have published notes about Brecht, giving in whole or in part the picture which they have created of him. The characteristic feature is that his closest friends have mainly reported on his work and its consequences. The conception of Brecht is not simply a private individual, but the entirety of talent and output, results and experience, changing ideas, plans, works, and world-wide effects, all of which are linked with his name.

In this volume friends of his youth have their say: Hanns Otto Münsterer and Caspar Neher, who later became a well-known stage designer participating in many of Brecht's productions.

Writers describe Brecht:

Arnolt Bronnen, who after early years of friendship took a diametrically opposite road;

Lion Feuchtwanger, who helped the young playwright, who later in exile published the magazine "Das Wort" together with Brecht and Willi Bredel, and who in California wrote *The Story of Simone Machard* together with Brecht;

Günther Weisenborn, who collaborated with Brecht on *The Mother*, based on Gorky's famous novel:

Sergei Tretyakov, who informed Brecht about the development of revolutionary Soviet culture.

Then there are colleagues like Anna Seghers, Arnold Zweig, Johannes R. Becher (Minister of Culture of the G.D.R. from 1954 until his death in 1958), Konstantin Fedin, who delivered the laudation when Brecht received the International Lenin Peace Prize in Moscow in 1955, and Vladimir Pozner, who worked with him in Hollywood and in Berlin.

There are the younger authors who learned from Brecht, like the Swiss playwright and novelist Max Frisch, novelist Erwin Strittmatter, poet Günter Kunert.

Literary critics and theatre people give their view-points: Herbert Jhering, who awarded Brecht the Kleist Prize in 1922 and whose theatre criticisms helped to establish Brecht; the essayist Walter Benjamin, who said, "My agreement with Brecht's output is one of the most important and reliable points of my entire position"; Berthold Viertel, director, author and critic; Bernhard Reich, director in Munich and Berlin, who moved to the Soviet Union in 1928;

Wieland Herzfelde, founder and manager of the Malik publishing house; Max Schroeder, critic, after 1947 chief editor of the Aufbau publishing house, Berlin, which published Brecht's works; Paul Rilla, literary critic of whom Brecht thought highly; Ernst Schumacher, who made a considerable contribution to Brecht research with his weighty work, "The Dramatic Experiments of Bertolt Brecht 1918 to 1933", published in 1955, and other works; Werner Mittenzwei, also author of profound works on Brecht; Lotte Lenya, the actress, and actress Angelika Hurwicz, who played the main part in Brecht's production of *The Caucasian Chalk Circle* in Berlin in 1953.

Contributions come too from close collaborators like Elisabeth Hauptmann, who edited his published works; Ruth Berlau, former actress at the Royal Danish theatre; Käthe Rülicke, assistant in the Berliner Ensemble, today theatre expert and university teacher; Manfred Wekwerth, director and theatre theoretician; and a number of members of the technical staff of Brecht's Berliner Ensemble.

The composers Hanns Eisler and Paul Dessau, who worked together with Brecht for many years, and provided the music for many of his texts, also make their contribution; as does Bernard Guillemin, from the magazine, "Die literarische Welt", much the most marginal of all the authors represented here who, in an interview, provided Brecht with the opportunity to make a number of informative statements.

The selection which is presented here, which had to conform with the limitations imposed by a whole series of volumes, is a shortened version of the original German edition of 1963, with some changes and some additions. Even a much more extensive selection could only include a small part of what is worth saying. Much has not yet been put on paper, or is unavailable for other reasons; later editions will be able to give a wider range. Finally, many works have not been included since they overlapped, both in theme and message, with some of the present contributions.

The various portions of this book cover a wide range. They vary according to the character of the author, his aptitude for observation and writing, his standpoint, his position in time and place, and the fidelity of his memory. All the authors, however, offer indirectly a picture of their own persons and the prevailing circumstances, thus strengthening or making relevant what they say. Some of them sketch only a detail, others cover larger biographical, literary and historical connections. And like overlapping sketches which show various movements and changes, these individual accounts come together to give a portrait. Important features of Brecht come strongly into the foreground and are clearly seen. One instance is the greatness and persistence of his will. And some authors agree that he was a fascinating man and a wonderful writer, the greatest of our age or the greatest altogether.

Brecht was one of those whom he describes in a poem as improving "those who see them, and whom they see." And they serve us all, particularly "since we know that they live and change the world."

Leipzig, 1963/1973   H. W.

Translator's Note

A particular difficulty in preparing this volume was that Brecht's works, both in prose and verse, are frequently quoted by the contributors.

In the absence of any standard Brecht text in English, I have found it necessary to render all such passages into English in my own version. The aim throughout has been to provide the clearest possible working translation, corresponding closely to the German original.

In a very few cases, allusions in the text which might be unclear to non-German readers have been explained shortly in brackets; all such insertions are clearly marked.

All contributions have been translated from the German including three originally written in other languages: the essays by Vladimir Pozner (French) and Konstantin Fedin and Sergei Tretyakov (Russian).

The titles of all plays, poems and other works by Brecht have been translated into English for ease of reading. These titles are not always identical with those used in some English translations. A short list of those titles which might cause confusion is given with the German original.

Household Homilies	Hauspostille
Lute Primer	Klampfenfibel
German Marginal Notes	Deutsche Marginalien
In the Jungle of the Cities	Im Dickicht der Städte
The Measures Taken	Die Massnahme
The Fear and Misery of the Third Reich	Furcht und Elend des Dritten Reichs

J. P.

Lion Feuchtwanger
Bertolt Brecht Presented
to the British
1928

I.

At the turn of the year 1918–1919, soon after the outbreak
of the so-called German Revolution, a very young man appeared in my Munich apartment. He was slight, badly
shaved, shabbily dressed. He stayed close to the walls, spoke
with a Swabian accent, had written a play, was called
Bertolt Brecht. The play was entitled *Spartacus*.

Most young authors presenting a manuscript point out
that they have torn this work from their bleeding hearts:
but this young man emphasised that he had written *Spartacus*
purely in order to make money.

At that time expressionism was the great fashion in German theatre, and our young playwrights tore open their
breasts to produce long and echoing dramatic declamations
which preached that social institutions were bad, but that
man, on the other hand, was good.

There was nothing like this in the manuscript of nine-
teen-year-old Bertolt Brecht. It was, in fact, a speedily
scribbled dramatic ballad telling of a soldier returning from
the war to find his girl pregnant by another; to be thrown
out by her money-grubbing parents; to incite to revolution
the workers in the inns and streets of the proletariat; to
storm at their head the newspaper quarter. After this, the
manuscript became diffuse; several versions existed.

The most characteristic version related how the Girl stood
by the Soldier during the struggle: now that she was his he
left the revolution to look after itself, took with him the
Girl, slightly shop-soiled, and departed. He was now sated,

and revolution was something for the hungry; he left for home, where a broad white bed was waiting.

That was the content, expressed in a very unliterary way, of *Spartacus*. The characters spoke a non-fashionable, wild, strong, colourful language, not something read in books, but heard from the people.

I read this ballad-like play, and I telephoned the shabby man to ask him why he had lied to me: he could not possibly have written this play just because of poverty. The young author became very excited, and shouted at me in a dialect that became almost incomprehensible. He declared that he certainly had written this play solely for the money; but he had another play which was really good, and he would bring me that. He brought it to me: it was called *Baal*, had nothing to do with the god of this name, but proved to be much wilder and more chaotic, and a very fine affair.

But the manuscript of *Spartacus* had unpleasant results for me. In spring of that year, a Soviet government was proclaimed in Munich. It lasted for only a short time, and the city was then re-occupied by White troops. The homes of intellectuals were searched. Soldiers armed with revolvers and hand grenades entered my apartment, ordered me to open the drawers and the cupboards; and the first thing to fall into their hands was a manuscript entitled *Spartacus*. At that time things were not exactly easy for people in Munich; guns went off easily and hundreds were killed. The affair of the *Spartacus* manuscript could have ended badly for me; but the group of soldiers included a few students from Düsseldorf who had seen plays and read books which I had written; I was able to make clear to them that this *Spartacus* was not propaganda material.

Later, incidentally, when I managed to insist upon a production of *Spartacus*, I persuaded Brecht to call it *Drums in the Night*.

The writer Bertolt Brecht, born in 1898 in the small town of Augsburg, looks anything but German. He has a long, narrow head with protruding cheekbones, deep-set eyes, black hair growing low over his forehead. He emphasises his internationalism, and from his looks you might take him for a Spaniard or a Jew — or both. But this descendant of German Evangelical peasants, wildly attacked by German nationalists, is so German in his writing that it is extraordinarily difficult to make him understood outside Germany.

He is more interested in the work than the finished result; more in the problem than the solution; more in the road than the goal. It is his habit to re-write his work interminably, twenty or thirty times, and then once again for each unimportant provincial production. He is not interested in a work being complete. Repeatedly, even if it has been published ten times, the final version turns out to be only the penultimate one; he is the despair of publishers and theatre directors.

If somebody points out an internal untruthfulness he has no objection to altering radically the work of a year: but he would not devote a minute to correcting a crude error in obvious probability. This correction he leaves to the director, or his secretary, or Mr X. He is more interested in the internal curve of his characters than the external curve of the plot. As a result the plots of his plays contain the wildest improbabilities. The externals are so casually set down that the lack of continuity and logic repel a large part of the audience.

Bertolt Brecht strives for classicality, that is to say strict reality. But the lack of external credibility makes him appear romantic, and all of his works have a certain appearance of the fragmentary.

He shies away neither from crudity nor from extreme realism. He is an odd mixture of tenderness and ruthlessness; of clumsiness and elegance; of crankiness and logic; of wild cries and sensitive musicality. He repels many people, but anyone who has once understood his tones finds it hard to drop him. He is disagreeable and charming, a very bad writer and a great poet, and amongst the younger Germans undoubtedly the one showing the clearest signs of genius.

3.

Bertolt Brecht has made an invention which he calls epic drama. He gets very angry if you ascribe this invention to his lack of a sense of construction. The content of this invention is that he rejects all tension in drama, that he regards as inartistic the creation of antithesis and tension or any practically constructed plot.

In fact Brecht's epic theatre, in contrast to the French theatre, destroys any tension by announcing in advance, naively and clearly, what is going to happen. According to Brecht the important thing is that the public should, for heaven's sake, not get involved. Any tendency on the part of the audience to participate vicariously in the fate and the life of another must, according to Brecht, be banished.

What is important, according to Brecht, is that the man in the theatre should simply observe the events on the stage, craving for knowledge, craving for noise. The spectator should watch the course of a life. He should draw his conclusions, reject, agree, but for heaven's sake not have any sympathies. He should observe the mechanism of an event like the mechanism of a car. It is by no means necessary for the spectator to see a whole play. Since he is informed from the start about the various phases he can decide for himself whether he wants to see how the hero behaves in this or that difficult and interesting situation, how he fights, how he changes himself or others, how he relates to the mass, either becoming absorbed in it or holding his own against it, how he swims with the stream or against it, how he dies.

4.

The central point from which Brecht starts is probably the ballad. He has published a collection of ballads under the title *Household Homilies*, tales of life both great and small, presented in a popular and original manner, wild, impudent, bigoted, cynical. In these poems some persons and some feelings are seen for the first time and expressed for the first time.

It is probably not easy to convey the music of these verses in another language, but I believe that the character of this poetry is accessible to non-Germans; and I do not conceal my conviction that apart from Kipling, Brecht is the leading ballad writer of our times.

Amongst Brecht's plays, the comedy *Man is Man* is perhaps most easily comprehensible for wider circles. This play depicts the transformation of Galy Gay, a packer, into a soldier of the Indian Army. A machine-gun squad of an Indian regiment has lost its fourth member during a burglary, and in order to hush up the burglary has to get its fourth man back by hook or crook. For this purpose the three soldiers transform the harmless packer Galy Gay, a man who cannot say no, into their fourth man, Jeraiah Jip, soldier of the Indian Army. Working from the inside they re-arrange Galy Gay the individual into a mass-person, and do it so that finally he really is no longer Galy Gay the packer but Jeraiah Jip; when the real Jeraiah Jip appears unexpectedly and belatedly, his substitute sends him to the devil.

The superficial circumstances of the plot are fantasy; the city of Kilkoa in which the action takes place is something invented in every respect by someone from Augsburg; the soldiers have been borrowed in a completely childlike way from Kipling; and a central role is played by an unusually silly joke about an artificial elephant. Nowhere is there a trace of apparent probability, every illusion is destroyed in a primitive manner. But the inner logic of the transformation of the man Galy Gay is convincing; when the live Galy Gay holds the funeral oration for the dead Galy Gay, I know of no scene by a living author which can equal it in greatness of grotesque-tragic invention and basic grasp.

5.

The writer Bertolt Brecht has so far not been successful in Germany. Progressive theatres and large experimental provincial theatres present him, and he is a favourite subject for the literary world. It is not particularly easy to read your way into him, and to translate him is certainly very difficult. But I believe it is worth-while.

Hanns Otto Münsterer
Recollections of Brecht
in 1919 in Augsburg
1959

To date, little has become known about Bert Brecht's youth, and even the laconic data which re-appears as a stereotype in commemorative articles and biographies is extremely unreliable. Although he was already convinced at the age of eighteen of his future greatness as a dramatist — "I can write, I can write plays which are better than Hebbel's and wilder than Wedekind's," he noted in his diary in October 1916 — it is not very easy to determine the point at which this high degree of self-confidence was objectively justified by results. I am convinced that the decision came in 1919. This was perhaps the richest period of all in Brecht's work, though it had not yet led to a firm decision politically.

The young writer already had a respectable body of work to show in 1918. In August, after months of work, a first version of *Baal* had been completed, and the *Ballad of the Pirates*, written in the same summer, presented a glowing picture of the simple, close-to-nature life of asocial elements.

But in the autumn came military call-up, and service as a medical orderly in Station D of Augsburg Hospital; the duty was not too onerous, but it was a strict bridle for one possessed by a passion for liberty, one bursting all bonds. But now this fetter was cast off, the world lay open, life could commence.

The beginning of 1919 was marked by the revolution. Leaflets were burned in the streets of Augsburg, and on January 10th a squad of sailors rallied here too. The name of Spartacus was heard.

Quite naturally, the unrest of these days affected us too; on January 16th we visited the most varied political meetings, finally landing, late at night, in the company of Fechenbach, Eisner's secretary. Things were not very polite in the meeting halls: there was a run on gallery seats from which you could, if necessary, spit on the heads of the speakers.

One day later the news of the murder of Karl Liebknecht and Rosa Luxemburg trickled through. Despite our excitement, for our hearts beat for the left — less from political conviction than from youthful idealism — the first collection of Brecht's poems was being brought together just then under the title *Lute Primer*. Caspar Neher tirelessly provided glowing water colours: Baal playing the guitar, Orge with the soaped rope, the dead soldier's ghastly marches with drums and flags in the blue spring sky, and violet shipwrecks.

Brecht surprised us almost daily with new verses, some of which were found worthy of a place and others rejected. There was, for instance, a poem about a cabin boy reporting on his travels between Hamburg and Pernambuco, and turning after each verse to his audience with a shrill "Are you coming too?"; the poem on the fraternal tree, dedicated to the younger Walter, comparing the two brothers to a tree with two crowns springing from a single root; a poem referring to Li Tai Peh the poet: "70 devils could not tempt him. Li Tai Peh can pray in 70 tongues, in 70 tongues Li Tai Peh can curse"; and the *Dead Soldier* containing with reversed repetition at the end, the wonderful verse *Each estate has got its duty / The musicians make a row / The pastor makes a pious face / And the doctors make you fit for the front*. If my memory is correct, *Marie A.*, Brecht's most famous poem, was created during those days.

The murder of Kurt Eisner on February 21st ushered in the Soviet period in the political field. In the following stormy night in Augsburg we were present at the street fighting and helped to carry away the dead and wounded, but Brecht experienced the events in Munich. He stayed there in appallingly middle-class student digs full of plush-covered furniture, and wrote, in three days, a new play called *Spar-*

tacus. It was designed simply as a box-office hit, and Brecht himself thought it was not much good compared to *Baal*. In March he submitted it to Lion Feuchtwanger who, as the dramatist of the Kammerspiele Theatre in the Augusten Strasse, had an important word to say.

Feuchtwanger was so impressed by the very young author, and by Thomas Kragler, the hero of his play, that he immediately himself wrote a play called "Thomas Brecht", which was announced for the 1919–20 theatre season, though in the published edition it was entitled "Thomas Wendt". Brecht's play, however, took more than three years to reach the stage; it was only on September 29th, 1922 that *Drums in the Night*, as the play was now called, was produced for the first time, and won the Kleist Prize.

The "box-office hit" turned out to be the best play of its time about returning soldiers, and remained the best after the Second World War. It is known that Brecht later regretted the deplorable nature of his hero who, at the decisive moment, abandoned his comrades on the barricades in order to go to bed with his re-won girl. It is true that this is the shabbiest of all possible solutions, but at the same time it is the most vital one.

In fact vitality was the great slogan of those days, in which Brecht started working on *Baal* once again. On May 2nd, not long after the White troops had marched into Augsburg, Brecht read us the new version, in which almost the entire first section of the earlier version had been omitted. A few days later he made further far-reaching changes. The scene in the Hotel Continental was replaced by the carters' inn, even the abduction of Dechant — later she was called Sophie Barger — was cut, the three seduction scenes, including one intentionally shown as a renunciation, were combined and linked and motivated by hurdy-gurdy music, and finally the bull and procession scene was introduced. Every day there were changes and re-groupings, and finally the play was to be prefaced by the cynical motto *Cacatum est. Non pictum.*

Baal had a great influence on our life, the whole summer of 1919 pulsed with "Baalish worldliness", but the contrary was also true: the play itself received much from the life of those times. Naturally it is not a case of the reproduction of real events, it is not a *roman à clef* but it is perfectly true that the atmosphere of old Augsburg shows through everywhere. There is Brecht's garret in the Bleich Strasse with the table heaped with manuscripts, the hazel bushes along the Lech river, the birch twigs which decorate the houses on Corpus Christi; and the grubby inns in the Graben and Heddenbach. Some of the figures too have the features of life in those days, and in some of the dialogue there is no great gap between historical reality and poetic exaggeration. The ballad about the adventurer *dancing through hell and whipped through heaven* or the lullaby with the brutal lines *As you swim downwards / with rats in your hair / the heavens above / stay as fine as they were* were sung during the nightly orgies of Brecht's circle in Gabler's tavern just as in the brown halls and pot-rooms of *Baal*. The Wolfszahn, a meadow between the rivers Lech and Wertach, with its tall old trees, lush grass and willow thickets where we bathed and lazed in the sun, witnessed the same wonderful chatter with which Baal *lured to the trough* his friends and his women. At that time there were even wheat fields practically in the centre of the town at Lechhausen. Of course the sky elsewhere is blue, orange or violet, and the nights everywhere are clear and star-spotted, causing the blood of young people to rise higher: but we experienced this in Augsburg.

Amongst my most beautiful memories of this period are the nightly rambles through the old town, along Brunnlech and Graben, Pfannenstiel and Lueginsland. There Brecht sang to a guitar, all the strings of which were missing, his *Heaven for the Disillusioned: Halfway between night and the morning / Naked and cold amongst stones / Under cold mist finding refuge / For the disillusioned this will be heaven.* Or perhaps a cantata, practically an opera, would be improvised about the beautiful May night, and his friend Orge, acting as director, would wave his arms grandly, driving an imaginary orchestra to a wild furioso. And often too we clambered over the fences on top of the town wall, and serenaded the Augsburg beauties. Brecht with guitar, a friend with violin, a third with a lamp on a long pole. We would sing Goethe's "Rat-catcher" and a few songs by Wedekind, for instance "Galathea", the "Garden Tower", the "Weathercock", or the fine cuckoo-call ("Disappointment II") with the overwhelming final lines "So man becomes a Croesus of reason / But beggar-poor through its gifts", for which Brecht had invented the music.

Amongst Brecht's own poems few were as suitable for these serenades as *The Old Man in Spring* who found no cause for envy, because as he said *When I was young and very gay / Spring was much better than now / Pretty girls were much prettier than today / That's the only thing that makes us oldsters glad.* And amongst these poems which have probably been lost for ever there were real treasures: *Of all the girls long gone and now forgotten / I know that when I kissed them they were good / Only of one, the one I loved the best / I know it not.*

That is how we spent our nights. During the hot afternoons we swam in the Lech, lay in the grass, and climbed trees, as is testified by *The Gospels* written at that time: *On swimming in Lakes and Rivers* and *On Climbing Trees.*

One of our particular pleasures was provided by the "Plärrer", a small-scale fair, held twice yearly on the small drill ground across the Wertach river. The swing-boats were one of our passions. Brecht declared that nobody who used the swing-boats could be a philistine; in his play *The Fat Man on the Swing-Boat*, written in 1918, he tried to depict the "skin-changing" of a previously sober citizen caught up in the tumult of a fair. Riding the swing-boats with a girl, he said, was just as good as the culmination of love. Late at night we would then march in a ragged file through the sleeping streets of the old town; and Brecht, a great Wagnerparodist, improvised a Tristan-like aria to Ina, his Alsatian bitch.

It is hard to grasp how this life of apparent idleness could be combined with really concentrated work. A laconic diary note gives a hint: "We stand together on the Lech bridge at eve, below the darkening meadows, while the town is wonderfully outlined in the blood-red of the sinking sun." And the diary continues: "Brecht is writing." In fact he had to note his ideas literally as he walked, since such a fill of dramatic plans presented themselves. At the end of May he spoke of *Condel*, a tragedy, considerable parts of which were completed. This, it is true, was still strongly influenced by Büchner. In June Brecht worked together with Jacob Geis, then the literary editor of the National Theatre, on a comedy intended to make money, and therefore lavish in its concessions to the taste of the public. On July 22nd the scenario for *Herr Makrot* was drafted in my cottage in Pasing.

We may regret that these plans and sketches were later abandoned, but in view of the completed works we can bear the sorrow. The position is different with regard to the loss of two plays on which Brecht worked almost the whole year, and at least one of which had reached practically final form by December 1919. One of these plays was first called *David, or the Agent of God,* later changed to *Absalom and Bathsheba.* The story was taken from the Bible, which Brecht read again and again, and the style of which he utilised in various works. David is, despite all immorality described in the Bible, a man of God. The opening scene shows Absalom in the castle yard, listening to the rather disreputable tales about the aging king's tricks, told by soldiers of the castle guard. Then David, a huge silhouette, appears above, upon the wall. "I will hold a reckoning with my son Absalom." Silence. Curtain. This was an exposition which Brecht could not have presented more effectively in his years of mastery. The poetic climaxes were a conversation between Absalom and the trees, and a tender love scene when Bathsheba fled from David to Absalom, whom she loved, in his camp. Since the relationship between Absalom and Bathsheba was given the central position, it was naturally very difficult to work into the play David's tricks, as described in the Book of Samuel, designed to ascribe to Uriah the paternity of the baby awaited by Bathsheba; today I can no longer remember how this problem was solved. It is certain, however, that years later I was still convinced that this play, upon completion, would have been amongst the greatest plays in German literature.

Much more complicated in construction was the *Summer Symphony*, which was constantly changed, and in which various layers were superimposed. The central point of this drama, almost completed at the end of the year, was the story told by Petronius of the widow of Ephesus, who intends to starve to death in the crypt of her deceased husband. Comforted by the gallows watchman, she finally, when the corpse of an executed man is stolen, provides the body of her husband to be hanged in its place. Brecht located the whole story in an indeterminate past, roughly pre-Reformation Germany. Wicked songs hymn sensual pleasures in a meadow at dusk, an advance version of Paule Ackermann sings *Lucifer's Evensong*, that hymn *Against Seduction* which later was to play a similarly provocative role both in the *Household Homilies* and the opera *Mahagonny*. In fact there seem to be close links with this opera altogether; the scene of action has become quite different, but there is a notable correspondence between the two plays in the break-away from all order under circumstances of extreme threat. The *Summer Symphony* would probably never have been staged; almost every single scene would have been enough to touch off a wonderful theatre uproar, such as in those days was provoked by such comparatively harmless plays as Wedekind's "Wetterstein".

Four one-act plays have survived from the dramas produced in autumn 1919: *The Dead Dog,* a dialogue between a king and a beggar mourning the death of his dog; *Lux in Tenebris; He Exorcises a Devil;* and *The Wedding,* which was the only one of these plays later to be produced in Leipzig. These plays are sometimes reminiscent of Karl Valentin, whom Brecht prized so highly, but also of Courteline and once even of Ionesco.

This imposing output of plays was accompanied by a real flood of lyrical poems, the harvest of that year. Some of them, such as *The Gospels, Marie A., The Ship, The Drowned Girl,* and *The Men of Cortes,* were the pearls of *Household Homilies.* Some poems which were artistically just as valuable have disappeared, others were of course chaff and rightly discarded. For a period Brecht had Negromania: a Negro scene appeared in *Baal,* but was quickly removed again; a few poems like the poem of the blissful woman, deal with Negroes, and Brecht rather liked to sing the verse: *This Negro was not handsome / And neither was he bossy / He did not take care of his looks / But the cops had him on their books.* One of the plans at this period, was for a Negro tragicomedy, about a sort of black "Marquis von Keith" who climbed to the top rung of society, but then fell.

The story is told that in later years Brecht was asked by a student of literature what his attitude had been in those days towards impressionism, expressionism, naturalism and symbolism; Brecht gave the stereotyped reply: "Didn't exist in Augsburg then." This is naturally little more than a joke; all these ideas were available, and were discussed by us, without, however, the almost incessant production process being governed by one of these tendencies.

Incidentally, there was almost no literary form at which Brecht did not try his hand. There were the wonderful ballads, such as the one about the mother of the missing boy, eternally waiting, with an empty chair always at the table for the awaited one; in addition he produced rude moralities, short and mainly very erotic novels, brilliant aphorisms, magnificent diary entries, and scenarios and librettos for operas and oratoria, which Brecht regarded as an unjustly neglected market for poetry.

Not only did Brecht create ceaselessly; we, his friends, were encouraged to artistic activity. Brecht wanted to force Orge Pflanzelt to write a book on a subject not yet determined, and Brecht suggested to me, quite seriously, that we should publish our poems jointly. The same spring Otto Bezold wrote his only story, but a really good one, "The Death of Manuel Linde", greatly praised by Brecht.

Caspar Neher, whose artistic ability could be doubted by nobody, even at that date, was begged day by day to provide new illustrations, with which Brecht's room was finally papered; for those with musical talent, Brecht provided texts which could be set to music, and operatic themes.

For his part Brecht willingly accepted from us ideas and suggestions for changes in his own work; there were occasions when one of our poems which was a failure provided him with the starting point for one of his own fine poems. Even at this early stage there were the first signs of co-operative work, in which of course Brecht took the undisputed lead.

Looking back forty years later it can be said that this year 1919, despite all its unhappiness, was a happy year, for us perhaps the happiest year of all, and certainly a happy year for German literature.

Arnolt Bronnen
Brecht Directs
1960

It was a stroke of luck for a director just starting: finding an author who had not yet started. Brecht could scarcely believe it: this man Bronnen had written three plays, in addition a dramatic novel, without thinking in the least that these plays might be staged, let alone considering how.

It was a stroke of luck for such an author to find a director at all; and now he had found a director who translated a play into stage directions the instant that he read it.

Dr Seeler, at that time still denying Brecht's genius because he, as a romantic, was revolted by the ceaseless literary activity of the man from Augsburg, had immediately grasped Brecht's other side. This youngster, who after twenty-four hours had completed in his head a precise non-Euclidean book of stage directions — stage directions with as many dimensions as the play had characters — was a real find for the theatre.

Seeler immediately charged Brecht with the job of directing the play, a decision which Brecht had never doubted for a moment. But there was a catch: Seeler had already got a company together for the play, and this could not be changed, particularly since Seeler could not pay his actors. There are naturally plenty of actors who will act for pay, particularly in such crisis periods; but where could you get actors who would work for nothing? The words "for nothing" rang unpleasantly in Brecht's ears. They made him suspect that Seeler would expect unpaid work from his director too.

The mortgages burdening Brecht's work as director were the actors cast as mother and son. Agnes Straub was to be the mother and Hans Heinrich von Twardowsky the son. Agnes Straub did not appeal much to Brecht: she was blonde, large, muscular, and had the sentimental touch of fleshiness. Twardowsky did not appeal to Brecht at all.

This descendant of a Germanised family of aristocratic officials was simultaneously Bronnen-near and Bronnen-remote. Bronnen-near in his tendency to exaggerated over-done intellectuality, Bronnen-remote since he lacked the barbaric temperament of those inhibited and oppressed. For Brecht both factors were without interest; for him Bronnen was nothing but the raw material from which he intended to mould the false revolutionary who explodes in the wrong direction. Here Brecht saw the similarities in the theme to his own *Drums in the Night*, and he intended to learn, while directing "Vatermord", important lessons for revising his *Drums*.

Where Brecht appeared you found certainty and deter-mination. This thin, pale, bespectacled man strolled about the various stages which Seeler made available — they had to beg their way from rehearsal to rehearsal, without know-ing in which theatre they would finally have the premiere — as though he had decades of practical theatre work behind him. At the beginning he fooled everybody, even the colos-sal Heinrich George, whom Seeler had provided to play the father. George was undoubtedly miscast in "Vatermord"; he was not the grumbling Viennese petty bourgeois broken more by life than by his son; he could not depict, through the collapse of a small suburban family, the collapse of a whole state, a whole system of states. George could produce explosions, but not the result of explosions. Brecht was look-ing here beyond "Vatermord" to the potentialities which George offered for future Brecht plays. He prescribed an under-cooled Brecht style for the Pomeranian giant, and was increasingly enthusiastic the less George resembled the nightmare figure of Bronnen's play.

George's reaction was different. He had the ethics of the player who wishes to become a great actor. He had the ability to visualise the part and to see himself; he could not be deluded when he noticed that George and the part did not fit each other. Brecht, who provoked Agnes Straub to hysterics, fought for George with embittered energy; but while Straub and Twardowsky accepted patiently the sadistic lashes of the young director, George rejected his enthusiasm. The rows increased from rehearsal to rehearsal. On the very day when Seeler rented the Neues Theater am Zoo and sent the notices about the premiere to the newspapers, George shouted down his director, pulled his script from the capacious pocket of his Teutonic Loden coat, swung it round his head like a tomahawk a couple of times, and then hurled it from the stage over the dark and empty rows of seats. It landed on seat 337 in the fifteenth row, where the disconcerted author collected it.

While George's 250-pound footsteps were still echoing, Agnes Straub collapsed in hysterics and had to be helped from the stage. Brecht announced: "The rehearsal continues," rolling his "r" a little more sharply than usual. But on the stage there sat only the unhappy Twardowsky, his face with its serious features resting on his slender hands, staring before him, incapable of hearing, incapable of speaking. Brecht grasped that this was his chance. He cleared his throat loudly, slammed shut his rehearsal book, loudly switched off the rehearsal light, said "Good day," and looked for Bronnen, whom he found sitting, upset, shrinking in the back row of the stalls. The director approached the author, his eyes gleaming in the dusk of the theatre with a satanic glow, which appeared to the author almost like triumph. Brecht said to Bronnen: "Congratulations. With that bunch it would never have turned out right."

Herbert Jhering
Bert Brecht
the Dramatist

1922

Never has the tension between the experience of an age and its expression been so great as it is at the present. This unproductivity did not become a judgment upon the epoch as long as the slackening was the natural reaction to the tautened nerves of the war years. People cursed the emerging generation without realising that they had had to fight harder than any generation for one hundred years. Not so much for their material existence. Not so much for their intellectual standing. They had to fight for something which had been denied to no generation except that after the Thirty Years' War: experience itself. The horrors of the last few years were not the collapse of a nation, but the inability to experience the elementals elementally. People's energy was so exhausted that they accepted apocalyptic events like everyday inconveniences. Pain is not the worst thing, but lack of sensitivity to pain.

It is only when we understand in this way the intellectual fate of the past few years that we can find contact to contemporary drama. The writers of today can only be understood when we feel that the spectral character of today is due to the fact that it cannot hear its own sounds, nor see its own grimaces. The writers were isolated, and attempted to project their language into the today, through areas pierced by no experience. This cramped situation was necessary, and had to be resolved in that moment when the times themselves began to resolve.

There can be no doubt that this process of resolution is in preparation. It began in poetry and continued in the novel. And now the miracle commences. Nothing happens by chance. But even those who felt with their nerves that the times wanted to emerge from their unproductive stagnation; those who felt in Bronnen the drive towards giving form and force to temperament; even these were overwhelmed by the intellectual change produced by the first deed of a genius. The twenty-four-year-old writer Bert Brecht has changed overnight the poetic face of Germany. Bert Brecht has brought to our times a new tone, a new tune, a new vision.

The artistic event is not that in his first play *Drums in the Night* Bert Brecht gives artistic form to contemporary events which were previously only talked about.

The event is that our times are the background, the atmosphere, even in those plays which are in no way contemporary in their theme. Brecht's nerves, Brecht's blood, are filled with the horror of the times. This horror exists as stale air and semi-light surrounding people and places. It thickens in the intervals and the pauses between scenes. It releases the figures and swallows them again. The figures are phosphorescent.

Brecht feels physically the chaos and the putrefaction. This is the reason for the unparalleled pictorial strength of the language. This is a language that you feel in your tongue, your palate, your ears, your spine. It omits links and opens up perspectives. It is brutally sensual and melancholically tender. It contains sordidness and deepest mourning, grim humour and plaintive lyricism.

Brecht sees people, but always in their relations to others. None of his figures stand isolated. For long there has been no writer in Germany who without preliminaries had the tragic necessity of showing how fates are linked, how people affect one another.

The signal of Brecht's genius is that his plays have ushered in a new artistic totality, with laws of its own, a dramaturgy of its own. His plays, starting with *Drums in the Night*, increasingly in *Baal*, and *In the Jungle of the Cities*, are new poetic planets. It must fall to a later work to show the laws which govern their orbits, the new feeling for space (this space stands threateningly behind people and supervises them), and to describe the new sequence of scenes. The task for today is to announce a dramatist who has provided the most shattering experience since Wedekind. He apparently shows putrefaction, and thus produces light. He is apparently cynical, and moves deeply with his cynicism. He is young and has already seen all the depths.

To feel the stimulating rhythms of his sentences you have to hear him presenting his own songs and poems with a guitar. He lets naked persons speak, but with a strength of language not heard for decades. When you hear the first words of his plays you know: the tragedy has begun.

The service to theatre history of first staging Brecht falls to the Munich Kammerspiele. Otto Falckenberg had the right ear for the gloomy melody of the play, but not in every case the actors who could carry it. Some of them, like the provincial Herr Gluth, blurred the earthy pictures of the language by uttering them — naturalistically — as though they had just occurred to him. Falckenberg had a feeling for the positioning of the characters, but not for the scenery — or not the necessary width of stage to arrange the characters in perspective (which is decisive in Brecht).

But Falckenberg had the actor for the main part. Herr Erwin Faber played the role of the returning prisoner-of-war, who finds his girl in the arms of a flashy black-marketeer, with a confused tension which is wonderful. Here we have an actor as relaxed as he is intense, who speaks no word which is not physically legitimate. He was not yet able to carry the dangerous ending in which the prisoner-of-war abandons the revolution for his unfaithful girl. This may, however, have been due to some unfortunate cuts, carried out by Brecht himself, and to the arrangement, which was rather smudged in this production. In any case here is an actor whom Berlin needs more urgently than the gentlemen from Frankfurt.

Apart from Faber, Herr Hans Leibelt played the black-marketeer with precision and a human undertone; Max Schreck, appearing once again in Munich as a guest from the Staatstheater, presented cheap and hammy blood-and-thunder.

Bernhard Reich
Recollections of Brecht as a Young Man

1957

In autumn 1923 I took over the post of chief director at the Kammerspiele in Munich, a theatre with artistic traditions and ambitions. The repertory for the coming season included *The Life of Edward II*, a free adaptation by Brecht and Feuchtwanger of Marlowe's play. Brecht had insisted on directing. I made his acquaintance in the theatre office.

At that time he was a slight man. The shape of his head gave him a dynamic expression. Deep-set threatening eyes. A poet? More of a thinker, an inventor, one who pulls the strings of souls and destinies. Conversations with him soon became filled with inner drama. He spoke very quietly, but he made claims, expressing these claims in paradoxical formulations. Absolutely categorical. He did not argue with the replies, but swept them away. He made it clear to his partners that he, Brecht, regarded all resistance to him as hopeless, and that he gave them, the partners, the friendly advice not to waste time but to capitulate right away. Was this attitude cunning, a pose, youthful presumption, or had he an inner right to it?

I read *The Life of Edward II* in proof. At that time I did not detect in this work the new, the Brechtian features, but I saw that it must be the work of a rare talent.

Logically enough the signs of artistic talent cannot easily be defined. Stanislavsky managed to take some steps towards a scientific definition of talent as an actor. He stated that it was a sure sign of talent if the actor, having found a genuine adaptation to the conditions and circumstances provided by the dramatist, then put them into practice in a shining, surprising and convincing manner. One might say that the talent of a dramatist is demonstrated, among other factors, by the shining, surprising and convincing manner in which he presents and completes the necessary progress of the plot. Brecht's play was packed full with expressions of this talent. More than twenty-five years have passed since I last read *Edward II*, but I still recall very exactly one particular scene. The ambitious Lord Mortimer, who wishes to fish in troubled waters, intends to create dissent between the king and his barons. He raises the question of "Gaveston". Gaveston is the king's favourite, of lowly rank, envied and hated by the barons.

At a session of parliament Lord Mortimer takes the floor, and the peers — and with them the audience — expect him to speak of Gaveston and his failings. But the clever demagogue tells the story of the conflict over Helena which led to the outbreak of the Trojan War and describes the fateful consequence of this war which came about for personal reasons: Troy was destroyed. This excursion into history, throwing a particularly sharp light on the shortcomings of the present, leads to an open outbreak of the conflict between the king and his barons. Mortimer has achieved what he wishes, and can allow himself a clever joke. Troy was destroyed but "Should Troy still stand ... then we would not have the Iliad."

The rehearsals directed by Brecht took a curious course. Brecht as director liked one of the actors: *ergo* he must be shown off to better advantage. Brecht as dramatist took a piece of paper from his pocket and wrote new lines for the actor. Director Brecht discovered that the intentions of the author could not be implemented stagewise. Next morning Dramatist Brecht brought altered and more suitable lines. The final rehearsal drew ever nearer, and Brecht grew ever more active, handing to the actors over the footlights whole rolls of new lines. If one of them protested, Brecht looked at him with such unconcealed honest amazement that he took the manuscript and got down to the job of learning the new text.

The demands which Brecht made on his actors were un-usual and strange for them. German actors attach little im-portance to formal actions such as eating, drinking or fenc-ing. They summarise them, simply indicate them casually. Brecht, however, demanded not only that they should be performed realistically and exactly, but also that they should be skilful. He explained to the actors that such actions on the stage should give the audience pleasure.

Pedantically he exposed at the rehearsals the plot of the drama, the basic events of each single scene, the chain of events. He believed that the spectator must be helped to find his way in the story so that he might understand without trouble the intention of the work. I recall Brecht's work on a scene which echoed Judas' betrayal in the biblical legend. One of the king's *entourage* hands over a disguised man to those who seek him by giving him, as previously arranged, a kerchief. Brecht repeated this scene for hours. He explained to the actors that the audience must see: this is a man who betrays, this is a scene of crass betrayal. He held up fair-ground theatre as an example to the players who, as actors of a refined and artistic theatre, felt themselves to be aristocrats of the spirit. Fair-ground theatres did their best to demonstrate the good and the bad to the audience, Brecht explained.

When an historical play is in preparation, the theatre workshops fall into a panic. They work night and day to produce imposing sets and fine costumes. Expressionism led to a radical simplification of the presentation of historical dramas by setting up a system of action areas on the stage, and clothing the players in geometrically figured costumes. Brecht rejected both these contradictory principles of decor — the mass of props smothered the spirit of the work, which was a fragile structure suspended in unrealistic space, they dissipated the reality-content of the writing which by its very character was flexible and hard to nail down.

Brecht primitivised the settings: a room was a room, and a king's chair was a chair, but the rooms and the chairs were kept in the style of the old German masters in their simple, merely suggested style. The costumes of the king and the barons were made of coarse dyed material: the spear carriers wore sacks. The staging principles for Pushkin's "Boris Godunov", urged by Alexei Diki in his article "Sovietskaya Kultura", have many points of similarity with that Brecht production of *The Life of Edward II*.

The actor on the stage displays a characteristic adaptation to the given conditions and circumstances. From the stalls Brecht calls: "Wrong, quite wrong." The actor and his partner stand there, bewildered and without understanding — what is wrong, why wrong? It is wrong, Brecht explains, since the actors have not grasped either the *unique nature* of the circumstances or the individuality, *this particular* individuality of the character. His maximalist demand at that time was a complete individual scenic embodiment of the dramatic figure.

The production was enjoyable, since sentimentality had been expunged and rhetoric almost overcome: sentimentality and rhetoric were the classic sins of German theatre. We appreciated the original and talented intentions of the directing. Today I realise this production provided a special and fruitful conception of the theatre. With rich fantasy of form the effort was being made to probe appearances to their depths, to see man as he is, and to judge him harshly.

In the following year (1924–25), Brecht settled in Berlin. To get to his studio apartment you had to climb five flights, balance your way over a sort of catwalk, open a massive iron door, and pass along a broad corridor. From the large windows you could look down upon Berlin. This meant that Brecht always had under his eye the roofs of the German capital, which he planned to conquer. Several factors spoke for the success of his plans. He was free of many of the illusions damaging to youth and its ambitions. He had, for instance, discovered that truth alone meant nothing, that alone it moved nothing — it must be implemented. But implementation was beyond the strength even of a genius: only if many give their help can truth win. Since Brecht thought at that time like a bourgeois intellectual, he believed that he must create a network throughout Germany of supporters and believers who would work for a new art in key positions in theatres, publishing houses, newspapers. He regarded himself as chieftain of this band.

In the bourgeois world the artist has developed the mania of converting the creative process into a mysterious process which can only be carried out successfully in sacred isolation, and which must therefore be carefully guarded from any premature external influence. Brecht, on the other hand, regarded writing as a very important, unusual, but absolutely profane undertaking.

On a long table pushed to the window stood a typewriter, open and ready for work, and many files containing material, mainly newspaper cuttings from the old and particularly the new world. When a visitor appeared Brecht regarded this as an event which helped in his work. He read to the visitor a particularly tricky passage, either trying out the quality of the work on him, or testing it with him. Sitting down right away at the machine, he typed the new version. Brecht gathered round him young people, collaborators. They collected material, discussed his plans with him, made suggestions, changes, improvements. In the published editions of his works they are named as assistants.

Brecht never concealed his opinion that art should earn its bread. Later he put this conviction in plain words in the mouth of Galileo Galilei: "... I despise people whose brains are not capable of filling their stomachs." It would be a scandal, Brecht thought at that time, if he had not soon got a car and a house in the country. But at the time his work only ensured him a humble livelihood. Literary circles recognised his great talent, but the public did not accept his plays.

Once he told me his plans for the comedy *Man is Man*, upon which he was working, and read me a few scenes. In the course of a conversation about the artistic quality of this work he asked me: "Will this play be successful with

43

audiences?" I said that it would not; many things in the play were, both in content and presentation, unusual and estranging for the audience. I illustrated my argument with examples of writing which pleased. Brecht ended the conversation with a long-drawn sighing "Yes," which under these circumstances could mean nothing except that he would, though reluctantly, try to adapt himself to public taste. A few days later he showed me a new version of the scene "compromising" with the public. It turned out, however, that those elements likely to estrange the public had not been modified in the new version, but radically sharpened. We laughed heartily about the failure of his attempt to make compromises in his work. Brecht could only write in the way he had to write.

An outstanding feature of the character of the young Brecht was his pleasure in research, in creative work. I had the task of directing "La Dame aux Camelias" in Reinhardt's Deutsches Theater. Dumas' play had been translated by Theodor Tagger. A comparison between the play and the book showed clearly that Dumas had aimed at flattering and cheating the theatre audience by giving a consoling turn to the ghastly material.

My intention of placing the basic material undisguisedly on show, contrary to Dumas, was strengthened by the impression made by Balzac's works which I had just been reading. I thought that in the first three acts I could accomplish this simply through directive interpretation, by removing the sentimental passages, by consistently and realistically showing the typical French provincial bourgeoisie. But I realised that in the last two acts the scenes and the text itself would have to be changed. I told Brecht of the difficulties. Brecht caught fire, declared that he would make a Balzac out of the miserable Dumas, wrote new episodes into the fourth act, and re-wrote the fifth. He did this simply out of pleasure in creative work, for he could expect no material reward. Legally the author of the translation was Tagger, and it was his name which figured on the programme.

Bernard Guillemin
On What Are You Working?
A Talk with Bert Brecht
1926

Bert Brecht lives in the west of the city, in a high, roomy studio right under the roof, but at the same time high above the roofs. He speaks a language which is certainly not polished but is studded with simple parables which come from the real and untranslatable stock, the fullness of the language itself. He speaks without the easy flow of the rhetorician; he is, rather, continually experimenting with expressions. Sometimes he speaks in a throwaway fashion, in a manner which eliminates the object of his disfavour.

But on the whole one gains the impression that he is one of those few people who, even when dealing with ideas, can still develop that intellectual and fantasy-filled politeness which has today almost died out. Perhaps it is only due to his politeness with regard to ideas that in the course of our conversation we were able to reach a joint result.

This result appears important enough to be mentioned prematurely at this point. It was reached when Brecht expressed his belief in both the insolubly chaotic nature of the material, and the overwhelming role of intellectual cognition in dealing with the material. The point had thus been reached at which irrationalism and intellectualism are reconciled. The supreme commandment for the intellect is to respect the chaotic as a non-soluble remnant and also as an overspilling portion of reality, and to adjust the fashioning accordingly. The presentation itself is governed almost entirely by the intellect.

The same applies to the attitude of the true receptor, who must always attempt to understand the work of art to that

45

last frontier where the chaotic begins. In this sense intellectualism is a method of the spirit, and irrationalism a characteristic of reality. The one sets a frontier to the other. But since, as we know, the frontiers of the spirit lie in infinity, any premature rejection of intellectualism is at the same time a misconstruction of all that is somehow perfectable in infinity; that is to say in the final analysis nothing other than an indolence inimical to fashioning when faced with the irrationality of reality. Finally it must be noted that I have intentionally translated into a language using the conventional terms what Brecht told me in his manner, in Brechtian "slang". The whole point of the interview is this interpretation which should serve a wider public.

"Am I in the wrong when I regard you both as a poet and a dramatist?"

"My poems have a more private character. They are designed for a banjo or piano accompaniment and demand mimed delivery. My plays on the other hand reflect not my private feelings but the feelings of the world. In other words, an objectively regarded matter, the opposite of feeling in its usual and poetic sense."

"This cannot always be recognised in productions of your plays."

"Nothing else was to be expected. They are mostly played quite wrong. They have produced the poet whom they think they see in me — something which I scarcely am outside my plays, and certainly not inside them."

"You thus reject the poetic participation of the author in his characters and events and everything concerning them which may be expressed in the play itself?"

"I do not allow my feelings to flow into the theatrical embodiment. This would falsify the world. I attempt a classical, cold method of depiction, based largely upon the intellect. I do not write for the scum who value having their heartstrings plucked."

"For whom do you write?"

"For the sort of people who come to enjoy themselves, and do not hesitate to keep their hats on in the theatre."

"But most people want their hearts to flow over."

"The only way to respect the audience is to estimate its level of understanding as high as possible. It is absolutely wrong to believe in the naivety of people who are already adults at seventeen. I appeal to the brain."

"I sometimes find lacking an intellectual penetration of your material. You do not make the happenings transparent."

"I provide the naked events, so that the public may think for themselves. That is why I need an audience with sharp senses, who know how to observe, and who enjoy using their own intellects."

"You don't want to make things easy for the audience?"

"A member of the audience should be psychologist enough to penetrate himself the material I offer him. I guarantee solely the absolute reality and correctness of what happens in my plays; I am ready to bet on my knowledge of human nature. But I leave the widest scope for interpretation. The meaning is inherent in my plays; it has to be extracted."

"But there is nothing to be said against an artist who, contrary to your method, makes his material understandable."

"There are writers who only provide the events. I am one of these. My material *is* understandable. I therefore do not need *to make* it understandable. There are also writers who, apart from the events but elementally divided from them, provide the theory. In this case the theory can be checked on the basis of the events. And finally there is a third working method which attempts to provide a mutual interpenetration of analysis of terms and of living material. I believe that only the first method can meet fully the idea of the drama."

"Of course. But in specific cases this can confuse the spectator: he can no longer find his way in the material."

"If this is so, then the contemporary theatre is responsible, which presents unclearly and mystically everything which is worthy of investigation."

"Do you wish to say that it is not the author but the director who must make the dramatic events understandable?"

"For the epoch in which the piece is played, yes. Real theatre plays can only be understood when produced. But there must be a break with the ruling fogginess including monumental fogginess. The foggiest thing which exists is a bad poster. I am for epic theatre! The director must disclose, quite soberly and factually, the events. Today the meaning of a play is usually blurred precisely by the fact that the actor plays his way into the heart of the spectator. The figures presented ingratiate themselves to the audience, and thus are falsified. Contrary to the present practice they should be placed before the audience quite coldly, objectively, classically. They are not objects for feelings; they should be understood. Feelings are a private matter and therefore narrow-minded. The brain, however, is loyal and relatively all-embracing."

"That's outright intellectualism. In my eyes it is a great achievement not to have fallen prey to the anti-intellectual currents of the recent past."

"Possibly. In any case I am not so frighteningly chaotic as people sometimes think. I limit myself in my plays to the plain material, but I depict only the typical, I select: that is orderly. Even if one of my figures moves in contradictions, this is only because a person can never be the same at two different moments. The exterior changes constantly force him to an interior regrouping. The continuous ego is a myth. Man is an atom constantly decaying and forming itself anew. What has to be depicted is what exists."

"But this result, in which the brain affirms the chaos in reality, you achieved . . ."

". . . solely and exclusively with my brains. And chaos only exists because our heads are imperfect. What stays outside we call irrational."

48

"You know that I cannot leave without asking you what you are working on at the moment?"

"I am involved in two works. The first is the *Biography of Samson-Körner.*"

"What moved you to do this?"

"Samson-Körner is a grandiose and important type. I wanted to nail him down for myself. The easiest way was to get him to tell me his life. I value reality very much. However, facts such as Samson-Körner can be counted on one's fingers: happy chances. The first thing that struck me about Samson-Körner was that he appeared to box in a completely non-German manner. He boxed factually. This has great plastic charm. The way that Samson-Körner, for instance, puts an ordinary bus ticket in his pocket is simply inimitable. This is why he is a very considerable film actor."

"How are you going about this work?"

"It is more a pleasure. I ask him to talk to me, and I attach great importance to his opinions. People's opinions interest me much more than their feelings. Feelings are mainly produced by opinions; they are also-rans. Opinions, however, are decisive. Only experience is sometimes more primary to a higher degree. But we know that opinions are not always founded upon experience."

"That too is strictest intellectualism!"

"Every action arises from insight. In the strict sense there is no such thing as acting on impulse. Here too the brain is at the back of things."

"And what else are you working on?"

"On a comedy *Man is Man.* This deals with the technical re-functioning of one man into another for a specific purpose."

"And who undertakes the re-functioning?"

"Three emotion-engineers."

"Is the experiment successful?"

"Yes, and everybody heaves a sigh of relief."

"Is the result perhaps — the ideal man?"

"Not particularly."

Elisabeth Hauptmann
Notes on Brecht's Work

1926

Instead of writing something about Brecht, something which I cannot at the moment do, I have selected from my old working notes a few passages. These passages may expose the inexperience of the writer, and other of her weaknesses, but also show her determination at that early date to take seriously, as seriously as these efforts deserved, Brecht's efforts toward a new theatre and his plays for this new theatre.

E. H. 1957

3. 1. 26

Plan for a comedy: *Inflation (Mentscher)*, a play about post-war youth. Schoolboys in the suburbs trade with motorcycles and with the copper which they collect from piles of old military telephones. The boys are old for their age, full of wise sayings and advice, and drive the girls too into dangerous experiments. — During Christmas B. has done some new work on *Charles the Bold*. His wretched end in the frozen-over dirty puddle, face downwards. None of those victorious with him recognises him. They really do not recognise him, so unrecognisable has he become.

18. 1. 26

For "Szene" magazine the "model" of Baal has been written up in the form of a newspaper report. The model for Baal, an "asocial element", is an Augsburg fitter. For *Jungle* too Brecht has written a "newspaper report"; it helps him to clarify the plot.

Re-writing the play for the production in the Junge Bühne

has given rise to a "dramatical biography". Brecht declared impatiently to a representative of the "Literarische Welt" magazine: "In the old theatre we are simply out of place, in the same way as Jack Dempsey could not show, in a bar-room brawl, what he can do. Somebody would simply bash him over the head with a chair and he would be k.o. . . . ."

7. 2. 26

Short visit to *Baal* rehearsal . . . Café scene. B. makes an effort to bring a little action to the "lifeless" table on the right . . . Death in the forest: the woodcutters should not treat Baal like a raw egg; Baal sees to this himself . . . When B. is not satisfied with something he has done, then he immediately sets to work and alters it . . . He says that Shakespeare was certainly his own best audience, somebody who mainly wrote things which entertained him and his friends.

29. 4. 26

Conversation about the importance of good beginnings for stories and plays. I am enchanted by the beginning of a story by B., *Too Much Luck is No Luck.* The first sentence runs: "We sat in cane chairs at Havanna and forgot the world." I find it wonderful, and I can also remember it. After an opening like that everything between heaven and earth can happen in a story. (Quotability!) Brecht draws attention to the opening scene of *Man is Man,* and wants me to acknowledge that it is a classic. I acknowledge it: I know it (almost) by heart. Thereupon Brecht declares that *Man is Man* is altogether a classic comedy.

30. 4. 26

Man is Man reconstructed again. (I believe for the seventh time, some scenes even more often.) And this from viewpoints which don't affect the theatrical effect. As long as the stage is not in sight, Brecht has little interest in this, but rather in the incomparably more difficult other points concerning human society and conduct.

8. 6. 26

Around Easter Brecht discovered a new lending library. "The Poor White" by Sherwood Anderson makes a great impression on him; after which he writes *Coal for Mike*. About the same time *The Grave of the Unknown Soldier under the Arc de Triomphe* (on the metaphysical soldier) and *Four Challenges to a Man at Various Times and from Various Sides*. (The big city = the thicket, the jungle, the battlefield.) Brecht wants to include these poems in the *Household Homilies*. The poem *8000 Poor People March upon the City* (for the magazine "Knüppel") "... must be included in another collection," says B., "which deals with the new man."

Plans and work: a revue for Reinhardt: *Parody on Americanism;* a novel: *Robinsonade in the City;* plays: *Joe Fleischhacker in Chicago (Wheat), Dan Drew (The Erie Railroad).*

26. 7. 26

The most important change of plans during the work happened while checking material for *Joe Fleischhacker*. This play was to be set in Chicago in a big way; as part of a series, *Entry of Humanity into the Big Cities*, it should show the rise of capitalism. For this play we collected technical literature, I myself questioned a number of specialists, at the stock exchanges in Breslau and Vienna, and finally Brecht began to read economics. He claimed that the practices pursued with money were very opaque, and he had to find out about the theories dealing with money. Before he made very important discoveries, at least for him, in this direction, he was aware that the prevailing (big) form of the drama was not suitable for depicting such modern processes as for instance the distribution of the world's wheat and the course of life of contemporary man, and in fact for all events with results. "These things," said B., "are not dramatic in our sense, and if they are 're-written' then they are no longer true, and the drama is no longer quite a thing; and when one sees that our world of today no longer fits into a drama, then drama does not fit into the world." In the course of these studies Brecht formulated his theory of "epic drama".

Back on 23. 3. 26 I had, incidentally, already noted shortly: Brecht discovers the formula for "epic theatre": act from memory (quoting gestures and attitudes), and works in his writing entirely in this direction. He performs the actions for himself. In this way the "demonstration scenes", as B. calls them, are created.

Oct. 26
After *Man is Man* had been produced, Brecht obtains works on socialism and Marxism and asks for lists of the basic works he should study first. In a letter a little later from holiday he writes: "I am now eight feet deep in 'Das Kapital'. Now I want to know all the details . . ."

Lotte Lenya-Weill
Threepenny Opera

1955

It was Elisabeth Hauptmann, Bertolt Brecht's reliable co-worker in the 1920s, who first drew attention to John Gay's "Beggars' Opera". There had been a new production of this in London and it had been a great success. Elisabeth Hauptmann immediately obtained the text and started on a rough translation. The German text, to which she devoted every free minute, she handed to Brecht scene by scene. Brecht was at that time deeply involved in work on a very ambitious play of his own which he had already promised to a director.

This, however, did not prevent him from plunging without delay into a new project; even then he delighted in starting innumerable things at the same time. He always had rough drafts, half-finished scenes and plays lying around, and he never threw away even the smallest piece of paper on which he had scribbled a few words. In Gay's play he met whores and pimps and beggars from eighteenth-century London, and they amused him: Why should he not make them speak his language, Brecht's language?

The idea pleased him and quite casually, practically for recreation, he began to fiddle about with a scene. He retained what he wanted, cut ruthlessly what he did not want, and wrote in new scenes as he saw fit.

He had always acted like this. His admirers spoke of adaptation and re-writing; his opponents called this method plagiarism, piracy, shameless robbery. He took his models where he found them. He did not care whether they were great writers of the past or contemporaries, whether Villon, Marlowe and Shakespeare, or Kipling, Gorky and Klabund.

During his whole life a sharp wind of criticism blew round Brecht's short-cropped head. Some said it was no surprise: faced with such a unique talent, narrow-gauge thinkers always pick holes. Others said it was no surprise: a dangerous charlatan like this must expect summary justice. A friend from those old days in Berlin said to me recently: "Every child knows that Brecht is not very particular with regard to intellectual property. Of course he pinches things — but he does it with genius, and that's what matters."

In any case Elisabeth Hauptmann showed an incredibly sure touch in bringing "The Beggars' Opera" to Brecht's attention in the winter of 1927-28. Here he found exactly the mixture of exoticism and actuality which he needed for his own production. The text was water on his poetic mills. Not much could be done with the original music by Pepusch. Brecht's language cried out for a new musical setting which could hold its own in tempo, drive, modernity and richness in low and high tones. This was a job which could not be done overnight. It must be undertaken without haste, without pressure of delivery dates. Only when Brecht had completed a few scenes and shown them to a director, and only when the director had become interested, did this question become acute.

And so Brecht and Weill started on their second joint work. (They had already collaborated in 1927 on *The Small Mahagonny*.) *The Threepenny Opera* was to be their first full-length work.

Weill and I lived at that time in the "Pension Hassforth" on Luisenplatz. We called it "Pension Grieneisen" after a well-known Berlin undertaker: pictures of dire and bloody stag hunts dominated our two rooms, and the furniture was painted funeral black. Weill had two or three pupils. He wrote criticism on the musical programmes of Berlin Radio in order to improve somewhat our sparse finances. I was happy to get an occasional engagement at a suburban theatre. Kurt sat down at his desk at nine every morning to compose. Incidentally, he scarcely used the piano at all, except

55

to give his pipe a short respite. When he was really immersed in his work he was as happy as a child. Fixed working hours were sacred to him: he would only interrupt them for a theatre rehearsal if this was unavoidable. Brecht rarely visited us in the boarding house; he preferred people to visit him. Kurt found this fine; only when he was composing did he prefer his own four walls.

Brecht was living at that time in an attic studio with overhead windows at the Knie. There were neither carpets nor curtains; but there was a huge cast-iron stove, a heavy table crowned with a typewriter, an easel with costume sketches and stage settings, and along the wall an overdimensional couch. On this couch, and on all available chairs, there sat the pupils of both sexes who always surrounded Brecht. Only Brecht himself, who in those days looked thin and fragile, did not sit down. He walked to and fro, cloaked in the smoke of his seldom extinguished thin cigar; first he would throw one of the seated pupils a lightning question; then he would hurl another a hurried throw-away answer. His deep-set brown eyes sparkled continuously. His narrow white hands gesticulated unceasingly, and translated each sentence immediately into the language of the theatre. Sometimes he was shaken by soundless laughter; then he dropped into a chair, clapped his hands on both knees, bent until his laughter was over, rubbed his eyes with the backs of both hands, and said: "Yes, that's life..."

When Weill visited him, when there was serious work to be done, his pupils soon left. Only Elisabeth Hauptmann and I often remained. Then the two started to discuss. In my whole life I have never met anyone who could listen so well as Kurt. He became all ear. With his thick spectacles he looked like a young theological student. He gave precise replies in a calm, low, deep voice, which appeared to have a trace of irony in it. Some people regarded as arrogance what in reality was only shyness. Brecht and Weill treated each other with the greatest respect even when their views differed; however, the relationship never deepened into firm friendship, such as that which later linked Weill with Georg Kaiser and Maxwell Anderson. Sometimes Brecht took up his guitar and played a few chords to give Kurt an impression of his idea. Weill noted these ideas with his small serious smile. He never said no; always he promised that he would try to work in Brecht's suggestion when he was composing at home.

Though we did not know it, a young actor had decided at the beginning of 1928 to start a theatre of his own. For this purpose he had rented the Theater am Schiffbauerdamm. This fine old house escaped destruction, as though by a miracle. It stands there today just as it did then, in red and white and gold, with its nymphs, tritons and plaster angels, with all its heavenly Kitsch. At that time the theatre was almost forgotten, though it lay in the best theatre district, only a few steps away from the lively Friedrich Strasse. Hidden behind the big business buildings it had fallen into a sort of Sleeping Beauty repose. The young and enterprising actor, Ernst Robert Aufricht, immediately started looking for a new play with which to re-open the theatre and make it famous at one stroke. He engaged Heinrich Fischer as literary editor and Caspar Neher as scene designer, called on theatrical publishers, maintained contact with the important agents, and visited untiringly the few cafés in which the long legendary Bohème of Berlin used to meet. In fact Aufricht first met Brecht in one of these cafés, the Café Schlichter. Of course, said Brecht, he was right in the middle of a new play, but it was impossible to say when it would be finished; and apart from that he had already promised it to another director. But wait a moment: he had another play in hand, something he had started on the side. Six scenes were already finished, and he had no objection to Aufricht taking a look at them.

A few days later, on a rainy afternoon, Aufricht sent his maid to Brecht's studio for the manuscript. Aufricht claimed later that it was half-sodden when he received it. Aufricht read it, his editor Fischer read it, and astonishingly enough they both wanted to put on the play. The first night should be at the opening of the theatrical season. Nobody appeared to pay any attention to the music. Aufricht told me not long ago that at the start there was no mention of music. Only much later when Brecht brought him further scenes he said that there was music to the play, composed by a certain Kurt Weill. Aufricht was dismayed. Could this be the Weill who was infamous throughout Germany as the enfant terrible of atonal music?

Finally Aufricht told Brecht that things would be all right. But at the same time he secretly asked a young musician named Theo Mackeben to take a closer look at the original music by Pepusch. If Weill were to produce an "impossible" score, then it would still be possible to fall back on a refurbished version of the old music.

The next thing that occurred to Aufricht was to move the date for the first night forward to August 28th. For B echt, who hated firm dates, this was a douche of cold water. There were excited conferences. It was agreed that Brecht and Weill must immediately leave Berlin. If they stayed in town they would never get through the work which still had to be done. Somebody proposed a small spot on the Riviera as refuge for the two of them. Immediately a number of rooms were reserved, and on June 1st we set out. Kurt and I took the express, Brecht drove by car to the south with Helene Weigel and his son Stefan. The Brechts had rented a house on the shore, and we had taken a room in a nearby hotel-pension. The two worked day and night as though demented, writing, altering, cutting, re-writing; they interrupted their work only to go down to the sea for a few minutes. I can still see Brecht today, paddling through the water with his trousers turned up, cap on head, the inevitable cigar in his mouth. I cannot remember ever seeing Brecht completely immersed. He must have been slightly water-shy.

I had been given the role of Jenny. Aufricht told me later that he had only abandoned the idea of using the old

Pepusch music after he heard me singing the *Tango Ballad*. Helene Weigel was to do the part of Mrs Peachum. So we studied our parts. When we returned to Berlin Brecht and Weill had practically finished their work. Engel, who was directing, could feel satisfied. Neher's sketches had been finished several weeks earlier, and the sets were by-and-large agreed upon. Now it was time for rehearsals.

And this was when the chain of bad luck began. I do not believe that there has ever been in theatrical history such a series of catastrophes shortly before the first night. All Berlin spoke of the fact that poor Aufricht was up to his ears in trouble. One misfortune followed another. Klabund was dying in Davos. His wife Carola Neher, who would have been the ideal Polly, had to cancel all rehearsals and go to him in Switzerland. Aufricht telephoned desperately in all directions to get a substitute. Finally he gave the part to the young Roma Bahn. Then the actor who was to have played Peachum — am I mistaken, or was it Peter Lorre? — quit the role. Erich Ponto was summoned from Dresden to take his place. Our Mack the Knife, the musical comedy star Harald Paulsen, and our Mrs Peachum, the popular cabaretist Rosa Valetti, never ceased complaining about the "dreadful play". Rosa Valetti, whose own repertoire was certainly not drawing room, screamed threats that she would never sing the "filth" in the *Ballad of Sexual Bondage*. On the last day of rehearsals she signed a contract with another theatre, convinced that *The Threepenny Opera* would stay on the programme for a week at the most. Helene Weigel suddenly had a gruesome idea how she should play the brothel-keeper — as a legless figure à la Lon Chaney in an old-fashioned wheel chair; then she got a swollen appendix, and her part had to be re-cast too.

Paulsen, who was extraordinarily vain even for an actor, wanted his first entrance as Mack the Knife to be particularly effectively prepared, in the text too. He requested a song which dealt with him alone, as curtain raiser. If possible the song should also mention the sky-blue cravat which he intended to wear. Brecht listened to him grumpily and said not a word. But the next day he brought the verses for the *Mack the Knife Song* with him, and asked Weill to write the music. We did not dream that this song would become a hit all over the world. It was patterned upon the songs of the ballad-singers, who performed at fairs and presented to the public in as complicated a fashion as possible the secret crimes of infamous criminals. Weill not only wrote the tune overnight: he also immediately discovered the barrel organ man who could provide the organ for the performance. His name was Bacigalupo. Paulsen was not permitted to sing the ballad himself. The task was given to Kurt Gerron, who had a double role, playing both Tiger Brown and the street-singer.

I can no longer remember who came backstage in those days to have a peep; but I can recall Lion Feuchtwanger exactly. His contribution was an excellent suggestion: it was he who invented the title *The Threepenny Opera*. Brecht immediately agreed, and the same day the new title was displayed in big letters outside the theatre. Fritz Kortner, Aufricht and Engel were all opposed to the big final chorus. "This must go," they said, "it sounds like Bach, and there is no place for Bach in *The Threepenny Opera*." But Weill did not want to cut it. Neher was in favour of the chorus being retained. "If you give in and cut it, then I am through with you," he told Kurt. The chorus remained in.

The dress rehearsal the evening before the first night was a farce; it lasted until five in the morning. Everybody was completely finished. We were all shouting and swearing at one another. Only Kurt Weill remained calm. Shortly before five the point came where I could start my *Solomon Song*. I had scarcely begun when the director shouted: "Curtains now! The song is cut. The play is far too long anyway."

We learned that Aufricht was already going around asking everybody if they did not know of a new play for him; he needed something new on the spot, otherwise he was lost.

Well-known Berlin theatre-prophets, as soon as they left the dress rehearsal, told all who cared to listen that Brecht and Weill intended to insult the audience with a wild mixture, neither opera nor operetta, neither cabaret nor drama, but a bit of each, with the whole thing bathed in an exotic jazz sauce: in other words it was indigestible. They suggested that the most sensible thing would be to cancel the play before the first night.

Up to the very moment when the curtain went up we had not a quiet instant. At midday we all assembled again at the theatre. We ran through the whole performance anew. This time things were quieter: nobody had the strength to get excited. To add to everything, we had an unusually hot summer that year, and the theatre was unbearably hot.

Late in the afternoon a cry of rage rang out again. The voice was unfamiliar to most, for it was the first time it had been heard so loudly. Kurt Weill had discovered that my name had been omitted from the cast listed in the programme. During his entire theatre career this was the first and the last time that Kurt completely lost control of himself. He created an uproar, but on my behalf and not on his. It was a good thing that I was there to quieten him down; somebody else would scarcely have managed it. I swore that nothing would prevent me from going on, programme or no programme.

So much has been written about the first performance that I can keep it short. It has become a legend. Up to the second scene, which plays in a stable, the audience remained cool and non-committal. They gave the impression that they were convinced in advance that the play would be a flop. Then came the *Cannon Song*. An unbelievable storm of applause. The audience was beside itself. From this moment on nothing could go wrong. The audience was enthusiastically with us. We could not believe our eyes or ears. Until the next morning we could not really believe in our success.

Then we read the first notices. They differed a lot. One critic wrote that he had slept throughout. Alfred Kerr, the best brain amongst the Berlin theatre critics, was rather impressed, but asked with a certain scepsis whether the future of the theatre really looked like that. Kurt Weill and I skipped through the notice to the last paragraph, with the sub-heading: "Who Was She?" It continued: "Judging from her accent she must come from Austria... An eye must be kept on her. Soon every child will know her."

After we had read all the notices, we felt that the time had come to leave our boarding house and move into a small apartment of our own.

Berlin was gripped by a *Threepenny Opera* fever. Everywhere, even in the streets, the tunes were whistled. A Threepenny Opera Bar was opened, where no other music was played. Immediately all sorts of scribblers imitated to death the "Brecht style" and the "Weill style", or what they understood by these words. What Alfred Kerr had prophesied for me became true almost overnight. Once when I was walking in the Tiergarten I passed a blind beggar. He called after me: "Fräulein Lenya, you only have time for blind beggars on the stage, eh?"

And the funniest thing was that all sorts of people now claimed sturdily that they had known from the very start that *The Threepenny Opera* would be a raging success. But I knew very well that most of them had not even been at the first night. Even today former Berliners visit me in my dressing room in the Theatre de Lys in New York and say: "I remember it as if it had been yesterday. That was a first night! Those were the days!" "Those were the days," I reply, and nod, though I know very well that the Theater am Schiffbauerdamm had the same number of seats twenty-eight years ago as it has today: not quite eight hundred. But what does it matter? When I think of those crazy days, I often recall the empty space in the programme: and I ask myself whether perhaps I too do not simply imagine that I was there.

Walter Benjamin
From the Brecht Commentary
1930

Bert Brecht is a difficult phenomenon. He refuses to utilise freely his great talent as a writer. Many charges have been made against him — plagiarist, trouble-maker, saboteur — and there is probably not one of these charges which he would not regard as a title of honour in his unliterary, anonymous, but noticeable work as a teacher, thinker, organiser, politician and theatre director. In any case it is undeniable that of all those writing in Germany he is the only one who asks himself where he should use his talents; who only uses them when he is convinced of the necessity; and who fails in every place which does not conform to this touchstone. *Experiments* 1-3 are places where he has used his talents. The new factor is that these places appear in their full importance, that the writer takes time off from his works for these cases, and, like an engineer starting to bore for oil in the desert, so he begins his activity at an exactly calculated point in our contemporary desert. In this case the places are the theatre, the anecdote, the radio: others will be tackled later. "The publication of the *Experiments*," the author states, "is taking place at a period in which certain works can no longer be so much personal experiences (the character of works), but rather be directed at the utilisation (transformation) of certain institutes and institutions." Not renewal is proclaimed; innovation is planned. Here poesy awaits nothing more from the feelings of the author, excepting those which have soberly allied themselves with the will to change the world. Poesy knows that the only chance which remains to it is to be a by-product of a very complicated process for changing the world. That is what poesy is here, and an invaluable by-product. But the main product is: a new bearing. Lichtenberg said: "What a person is convinced of is unimportant. Important is what his convictions make of him." And in Brecht's case this "what" is: bearing. This is new, and the newest factor is that it can be learned. "The second Experiment, the *Stories of Herr Keuner*," the author states, "represents an attempt to make gestures quotable." And when you read these stories you note that what are being quoted are gestures of poverty, ignorance, impotence. Only small innovations have been added, one might say patents. Herr Keuner, a proletarian, is a very sharp contrast to the ideal proletarian seen by the friends of the people: he is not full of soul. He expects the abolition of need to come in just one way: by the development of the bearing which forces need upon him. And not only Herr Keuner's bearing is quotable; exercise makes it possible for the schoolchildren in *Lindbergh's Flight*; and the bearing of Fatzer the Egoist is also quotable. And vice versa what is quotable about Fatzer is not simply his bearing, but just as much the words which accompany this. These words too need to be practised, that is to say first noted, and later understood. They have their didactic effect first, then their political effect, and right at the finish their poetic effect. To encourage the didactic effect as much as possible, to delay the poetic as much as possible, is the aim of the commentary, an extract from which follows:

I.

Abandon your post.
The victories are fought.
The defeats are fought.
Now abandon your post.

The defeats are ... less by him, Fatzer, than for him. The victor should not allow the vanquished to enjoy defeat. He should take this too, he should share the defeat with the vanquished. Then he will be in command of the situation.

Submerge again in the depths, victor.
The cheering penetrates to where the battle was.
Do not remain there.
Await the cries of defeat where they are loudest:
In the depths.
Abandon the old post.

Submerge again ... — "No glory for the victor, no pity for the vanquished." Poker-work inscription on a wooden plate, Soviet Russia.

Withdraw your voice, speaker.
Your name will be wiped from the tablets. Your orders
Will not be obeyed. Allow
New names to appear on the tablets, and
New orders to be obeyed.
(You who no longer command: Do not call for disobedience!)
Leave the old post.

Allow ... — Hardness bordering on cruelty is intermingled with politeness. This politeness is compelling because one feels why it is there. It should encourage the weakest and unworthiest (quite simply those at the sight of whom one feels one's heart) to the highest and most important. It is the politeness involved in sending the rope to the suicide, in a silence which still has room for pity.

You did not suffice
You are not ready
Now you have the experience and suffice

Now you can begin:
Abandon the post.

Now you can begin ... — "Begin" is dialectically renewed. It announces itself

You who ruled over the of-
fices
Heat your stove.
You who had no time to eat
Cook your soup.
You of whom much was writ-
ten
Study the ABC.
Begin immediately:
Occupy the new post.

The defeated does not
elude
Wisdom.
Hold on firmly and sink.
Be afraid! But sink!
At the bottom
The teaching awaits you.
Target of too many ques-
tions —
Take part in the invalu-
able
Teaching of the masses:
Occupy the new post.

not by soaring but by stopping. The deed? That the
man abandons his post. Internal beginning = to abandon something external.

You who ruled . . . — Here is
revealed the strength which
is awakened in those affected
by the Soviet practice of
moving around officials in
the most differing posts. The
order "start from the be-
ginning" means dialectically:
1. Learn, for you know nothing.
2. Deal with the basic matters, since you have become
(through experience) wise
enough.
3. You are weak, you are removed from your post. Look
after yourself, so that you
become stronger; you have
the time.

But sink . . . In hopelessness
Fatzer should gain a footing.
A footing, not hope. Solace
has nothing to do with hope.
And Brecht gives him solace:
man can live in hopelessness
when he knows how he got
there. For then he can live
in it, since his hopeless life

has become important. To
go to the bottom means to
get to the bottom of things.

2.

The table is finished,
  carpenter.
Allow us to remove it.
Use the plane on it no more
Cease to paint it
Speak neither good nor ill
  of it:
As it is we shall take it.
We need it.
Hand it over.
You are finished, states-
  man
The state is not finished.
Allow us to change it
According to the condi-
  tions of our lives.

Allow us to be statesmen,
  statesman.
At the foot of your laws
  stands your name.
Forget the name
Obey your laws, law-giver.
Comply with orders, order-
  maker.
The state no longer needs
  you
Hand it over.

Carpenter ... — Here one
has to imagine an eccentric
carpenter who is never
satisfied with his "works",
and cannot make up his mind
to deliver them. And if the
artist can take leave of his
"works" (see above), then
this attitude may be de-
manded here of the statesmen. Brecht says to them:
You are amateur, you want
the state to be your "works"
instead of understanding that
the state should be no work
of art, nothing for eternity,
but something useful.

Hand it over ... — And the
Lindberghs say of their
machine: "What you have

made will have to suffice." Closely approaching bare reality: that is the slogan. Poverty, those who bring learning say, is a form of mimicry which makes it possible to approach nearer to reality than any rich man can.

Sergei Tretyakov
Bert Brecht

1934

...He is a native German, but despite this the living mockery of everything which we foreigners are accustomed to regard as German. Can he possibly be a son of red-cheeked solid-boned Germania? The anaemic word "delicate" is bursting with health compared to Brecht's constitution. Instead of a jacket he wears a waistcoat, though one with sleeves. His hook-nosed face can be compared to Voltaire as well as to Ramses.

Berliners are people surrounded by patented machines and nickel-plated apparatus; what sort of a Berliner can Brecht be? The lift with which you get to his sixth-floor attic flat is so worn-out and dirty, so precarious on its steel cable, that you fear to use it. The lift rises with fits and starts, and you have to poke around for a long time with the key before you can open its door.

And Brecht's collar! A German is a person who first runs out of bread, then sells his crockery, and who only then abandons his stiff collar. On the streets I have seen unemployed Germans spending their last pfennigs to have their ties pressed by a curb-side presser. This is understandable, because without collar and tie you cannot get a job, particularly if you are an office worker. What sort of German can Brecht be? His neck is encircled by a crumpled shirt, his craning neck which is thinner than a human arm. His head sticks out with a snake-like movement, as though his suit did not clothe a man, but a rather dried and carefully rolled skin-coloured snake. This neck used to be encircled by a leather tie, but he presented me this with a really Georgian gesture, and since then has worn no tie.

A German is a man with a hat, a trilby with a broad brim. Brecht has a cap on his head — and what a cap! The brim is broken and turned skywards, as though a hurricane had blown out of Brecht's skull. On his nose he wears an antediluvian pair of spectacles such as nobody wears today — glasses with narrow steel frames. Brecht takes off his spectacles; his eyes, black pinpoints, dart to the tip of his nose and raising his index finger he holds a speech in defence of his glasses:

"Why should I wear heavy American tortoise-shell frames, which in addition are breakable, when these steel frames are strong and light? They wore glasses like this a century ago, and it was hard to find a pair."

Brecht guided me through the quiet old city of Augsburg. The Roman Emperor Augustus founded this city in the dense German forest. A memorial has been erected to him, which looks like a fountain and astonishes by its smallness.

In Augsburg they used to enjoy burning witches and heretics; and this was also the place which hatched and nurtured such vultures of banking as the Fuggers, who became rich from the metals of South America and from their commissions on the sale of papal indulgences.

In the city of Augsburg there stands a tall castle. The moat which surrounds it is empty. The waters of the river Isar have been diverted to the turbines of the factories. To get to the factories the water flows through a network of canals, sometimes with one canal above another in separate concrete channels.

Great chimneys reach into the sky over Augsburg, and the tallest of all — not only here but in the whole of Bavaria — is the chimney of the paper mill of Bertolt Brecht's father. It is 105 metres tall.

Brecht led me past a mighty cathedral, surrounded with the houses of clerics and canons. From the windows of the seminary comes the monotonous murmur of a theological lecture. Brecht surveys the cornices for bullet marks and relates:

"I started to train as a doctor. When I was a lad I was called up, and stayed on hospital duties. I bound up wounds and painted them with iodine, I administered enemas and gave blood transfusions. If a doctor had said to me: 'Brecht, amputate this leg!' I would have replied: 'As you order, Herr Staff Doctor!' and cut off the leg. If somebody had given the order: 'Brecht, trepan!' then I would have cut open the skull and poked about in the brain. In my immediate vicinity I saw how men were being rapidly patched up in order to send them to the front as soon as possible."

In the evening, at home, Brecht sings to the banjo with a shrill eagle's voice, to his own music, the *Ballad of the Dead Soldier*, which tells how a soldier is hauled out of his grave, patched up, and sent off to fight again.

This is the lonely and scornful cynicism of an intellectual, who sees the idiocy, has not the strength to hit out with his fist, and takes up his pen instead. He has got further than Voltaire, who gave the king sarcastic advice, but not as far as Demyan Byedny, whose verses were shouted by the Red Guards as they attacked the tanks of the intervention troops.

"In 1919," Brecht continued, "Leviné raised the banner of Soviet power not far from here, in Munich. Augsburg reacted to the red glow from Munich. The hospital was the only military installation in Augsburg, and it delegated me to the Augsburg revolutionary committee. I can still remember a Polish Bolshevik, Wojciechowski, on the committee. We did not have a single Red Guard. We did not get around to issuing one single decree or nationalising a bank, or closing a church. Two days later General von Epp, the 'pacifier', touched us with one wing of his troops. One member of the revolutionary committee hid out in my house until he was able to flee. Then Bavaria disappeared into the past. What came was Berlin, poems, plays ... decline ... loneliness."

This cynical, derisive eccentric, who managed to quarrel with the whole world, either got booed, or found himself printed in the school readers. In Berlin I saw how his play

Man is Man had to be removed from the programme of the Schauspielhaus after only six performances. In the respectable repertoire of this theatre Brecht's play was an uncalled-for and suspicious object with unclear aims.

Apart from Meyerhold's "Cuckold" this was the play which made the deepest impression on me. Across the stage strode giant soldiers, holding on to a rope so as not to fall from the stilts concealed in their trousers. They were hung about with rifles and wore tunics smeared with lime, blood and excrement. According to the story they were soldiers of a British detachment in India, murderous machines and marauders preparing for a frontier attack, an attack called "defensive war" in the play. And side by side with these three giants, shaped not only by the crust of their uniforms, but also by the logic of bourgeois laws, statutes and regulations, there dangled the soft-hearted and friendly petty bourgeois Galy Gay, "a man who cannot say no." The fourth mate of the three soldiers had "gone missing" after a joint robbery. Those responsible are being sought. If the fourth man returns, they will be unmasked, since a tuft of torn-out hair has been found and given to their commander. If the fourth man does not return, they will also be unmasked since they will be one short on parade. They lure Galy Gay, with beer and cigarettes, and convert him into this fourth man. They do not need him just once, but permanently. They have to drag him into a crime so that he disavows himself and stays with them. They persuade him to sell the regimental elephant. This fantastic sale takes place: two soldiers covered with a tarpaulin, and with the hose of a gas mask as a trunk, mime the elephant. The transaction has scarcely been completed when Galy Gay is arrested and charged with a triple crime:

"Listen carefully, man. Firstly you stole an army elephant and sold it, and this is theft; secondly you sold an elephant which is not an elephant, which is fraud; and thirdly you have no sort of name or papers and may be even a spy or a swindler, who gave a false name at roll call."

Retreat to the name Galy Gay has been cut off. His only salvation is to declare he is a soldier. But the wheels of justice, once set in motion, continue to roll. A salvo of blanks is fired at Galy Gay. A coffin is carried on to the stage and a nameless "unknown" found in the camp holds the funeral oration. Galy Gay, who sold the elephant, is finished with. What remains is a man without a name. There are two possibilities: either he is a spy who has crept into camp and must be shot; or he is a soldier, and then he must climb aboard the waggon, for the bugle is sounding to break camp. The unknown person answers to the roll call, the soldiers surround him, he puts on uniform. Then the last seconds of the play: on the footlights there appears a figure with a knife between his teeth, hung with hand grenades, in a tunic stinking of the trenches — the shy and proper petty bourgeois of yesterday, now a machine for murder. A man has been re-assembled. Shy and compliant as he was he has been laid upon the conveyor belt of capitalist logic, chopped by the machine, ground up and converted into a cruel, thrusting, laconic and obedient link in that machine of destruction called "capitalist army".

The intelligent middle-class Berliner does not go to the theatre to be made uneasy. He looks at the stage, and comments upon the action, like a kibitzer standing behind a card-player saying: "Yes, yes, quite right. No, that was unnecessary. Now why are you delaying?"

He stands superior to the plot, or at least at the same level. He cannot admit that suspicious and puzzling events are taking place on the stage which are possibly an insult to his solid respectability.

As a result, women stamped their heels, lawyers foaming with anger hurried from the theatre, hurling their crumpled programmes at the actors as they left. In the cloakroom a sobbing woman tore her coat from her husband's grip and went to a far corner to put it on alone. Her husband was unbearable, for he had watched the play without being nauseated.

The Russian writer Ossip Brick noted very cleverly that Brecht's works are always court cases, in which Brecht proves himself to have litigation-mania, and shows himself a skilful and cunning casuist. He is without compare when he conducts his case against bourgeois logic, on condition that the legal argument is based upon the precise foundation of bourgeois jurisprudence. In such a case he is unbeatable. So-called "beauty", so-called "truth", so-called "justice" and "honesty" and "progress", and all these other fine-sounding words so beloved by liberal aesthetes; all these phrases he drives into a corner, into a blind alley, rubs their noses in the horrors of the social system which produced them. He takes down the trousers of the solid citizens, and they can do nothing but howl, hit out in all directions, and slander Brecht, who has forced them to look at themselves in all their rapacious and stupid abominableness.

... Brecht's play *The Measures Taken* — the first with a purely Communist theme — places a court session on the stage. Four Party functionaries render account. The judge is represented by a chorus. The chorus delivers its statements, questions and sentence in ceremonious fugues written by composer Hanns Eisler. The various episodes of the story are enacted on a small podium (I would call it the *corpus-delicti* table), under the direction of Slatan Dudow, a Bulgarian, Brecht's constant assistant. The main figures are four illegal Party members who killed their fifth comrade (they had to in the interests of the Party) — a soft character who had acted without reflection, in accordance with his feelings.

One year later Brecht told me of a new idea of his: A panopticum theatre should be established in Berlin, showing the most interesting trials in the history of humanity. "The theatre would be built like a law-court. Two trials every evening. For instance the trial of Socrates. A witchcraft trial. The trial of George Grosz, who was charged with blasphemy because of his picture of Christ in a gas mask saying: 'Hold your mouth and obey orders!'"

Brecht is entranced by the idea. He thinks of more details:

"For instance, the trial of Socrates is finished. Then we have a short witchcraft trial, with armoured knights as judges sentencing the witch to death at the stake. Then the trial of Grosz begins, and the knights on the stage from the previous trial are forgotten. However, they are still sitting on the stage. And when the indignant prosecuting attorney attacks the artist who has dared to insult our meek and mild Jesus, then there is a frightful clatter, like applause from twenty huge samovars. The noise comes from the knights, moved by the way in which the defenceless Christ is being defended, and clapping with their iron-clad hands."

The Threepenny Opera brought Brecht international fame. The music for this opera, cutting and sentimental, was composed by Kurt Weill. The plot is taken from an English melodrama; Brecht provided the ironic poison strewn through the story. The remarkable success of *The Threepenny Opera* is due perhaps not so much to the fact that Brecht wrote it, but rather to the fact that Brecht is so cunningly masked by Weill's music and the adventurous story. The drama plays on two levels, one imaginary and one real. The imaginary level is illuminated by the sun of justice: the authorities catch a knave and murderer who hides in rat-holes. On the level of reality dictatorial power is in the hands of the murderous knave, and the police chief is his ponce and his assistant. Does it not resemble a parody on Al Capone, the Chicago boss?

I know of nothing that Brecht dislikes more than hokum. Whether sentimental hokum or pseudo-heroic hokum, Brecht always sees to it that the philistines and cowards preen themselves, and that the murderous knaves weep real tears.

When representatives of a film company, hearing of the success of the play, called upon Brecht, they began their negotiations something like this: "We want to produce your play as a fairy-tale, an enchanting fairy-tale." Brecht screamed at them with his tinny voice and threw them out.

Incidentally the applause earned by *The Threepenny Opera* was fully compensated for by the boos, whimpers and fury which greeted his other plays. Everywhere the philistines recognised themselves far too soon; they were naturally immediately insulted, and the play had to be removed from the programme before it had been performed, at the best, ten times. A philistine may allow a philistine type to be made fun of on the stage; but it is going too far if fun should be made of him, the philistine in the audience, the man who has paid for his ticket, going too far if he should be made to look a fool.

In *Saint Joan of the Stockyards*, a parody of Schiller's "Maid of Orleans", the expression "fouling your own nest" is used by stock-exchange operators who, by financial tricks, rob their colleagues of their last shirt. Brecht fouled his own nest when he turned to the Communist movement and presented his plays to a quite new public — a proletarian public.

"Brecht's turn to us came about like this," Johannes R. Becher says. "The slump began. Wages became lower. Bread became dearer. Brecht decided to write a play the hero of which should be wheat. The explanations of the economists were lies, useless. Wheat brought Brecht to Marx, and from Marx to Lenin. The play never got created. But a new Brecht got created, a Brecht who left no-man's-land and joined the ranks of the Communist artistic workers."

The Measures Taken made the newspapers uneasy; but then came *The Mother*, which Brecht based upon Gorky's novel, a play which, in an agitational manner, showed millions of proletarian mothers the road to revolution. Now the howling press fell silent, and the voice of the theatre critic was replaced by the voice of the policeman. *The Mother* was performed thirty times; then it was banned. All that was allowed was a formal reading on the stage. The actors lined up and began to read.

"Stop!" shouted the policeman in charge. "That is not a reading but a performance." One of the actors had turned his head towards another when answering a question.

The readers sat down on chairs and continued.

"Stop!" the same voice shouted once again. "You made

a gesture with your hand. That is not a reading but a performance. I prohibit any continuation of the reading."

Saint Joan of the Stockyards was staged in Erfurt. Half an hour after the performance began, the Nazis who had been whistling and yelling began to hit out with sticks, and the fighting in the auditorium made it impossible to go on with the play.

Brecht's room is a living sketch of his literary biography. On the wall hangs his dusty banjo, dusty because Brecht so seldom uses it these days to accompany his ballads. Next to the gramophone lie records of *The Threepenny Opera* sung by Brecht himself. On a huge sheet of plywood is a sketch, intentionally vague in outline, made by the artist who designed the sets for *Man is Man* in which there were giant portraits of the characters instead of a backdrop. A plaster bust of Brecht, looking as though broken from the mummy of Ramses. A jocular caricature in the form of a long vertical Chinese portrait, showing Brecht as Confucius.

Confucianism interests Brecht as a science of human behaviour; but on the bookshelves stand books on the science of human action — Lenin, whom Brecht reads aloud, or rather recites, with the unbounded enthusiasm with which some aesthetes recite the verses of Cicero or Virgil.

It is here that Brecht, the logical and abstract thinker, seeks the road to reality. It is not sufficient to deride reality — it must be changed. The arts in their previous guise are too static and too passive. This Brecht knows. But he seeks to revive the arts not by making more concrete and specific the materials from which the work of art is formed, but rather by making more concrete the effect of the work of art upon man.

Brecht claims that art is a department of pedagogics: it must teach. If people generally evade instruction, if they are insulted by each didactic tone, then this is simply because their schools have been places which deride the human brain. Real instruction is something desirable, and a person who receives instruction, who is made wiser and stronger, can

77

only be pleased. An example? The attitude in the Soviet Union towards study.

He fights against Aristotelean drama theories. He confronts the "theatre of events" with the epic "theatre of story-telling", and confronts the theatre of emotional "infection" with the theatre of intellectual convincement. He wants a clever theatre. He wants the ideas of struggle to be just as interesting as the emotions of struggle.

"Emotions lead people up the garden path," he claims. "Do not surrender, check the arguments against the action, seek out the roots. The essence of a play is not to send away the spectator after bathing him in catharsis, according to Aristotle's rules; the spectator should be changed, or rather the seeds of change should have been planted in him, seeds which must come to flower outside the limits of the performance. It should not be a circular performance in which everything is completed, in which the heroes and the villains are balanced; it should rather be a spiral performance, a tilted circle rising to another horizon, and a spectator who is thrown out of balance."

In *Saint Joan of the Stockyards* the dying heroine says these lines:

> *Make sure when leaving the world*
> *Not just that you were good, but leave*
> *A good world.*

In what does Brecht's strength lie? In his invincible aversion to hypocrites, villains, the sanctimonious, the respectable cowards, the egotists however they may express their egotism, either in greedy accumulation or humanitarian self-sacrifice. And particularly his disgusted derision for the modern gorillas — the fascists.

His latest play *The Round-Heads and the Pointed-Heads* is set in a country which is faced with the decisive battle between the poor and the rich. A saviour appears, who abolishes the division into rich and poor; instead he introduces a division according to racial characteristics — into pointed-heads and round-heads. The play tells us what then happens.

This is a direct satire on the National Socialists.

As an ingenious master of capitalist aphorism, Brecht treats very roughly the spruce and dapper verse of the symbolists. He starts a sentence with biblical ceremony, and then breaks off with a rude bang; he makes a stock jobber orate in Shakespearean blank verse, but the iambuses themselves stagger like a drunkard.

The military exactitude of traditional verse and exquisitely selected rhymes alternate in his writing with prose passages which have been raised to the rank of verse, and rhymes which are so poverty-stricken that they appear naked.

I have seen foam appear on lips of dignified German professors as they screamed that Brecht has no resemblance to a poet, that he had smuggled himself into literature like a fox: a man who rhymed "sein" with "Dasein" could not call himself a poet...

Brecht has made his way from the heights of intellectual equilibration through Lenin's writings to Communism, to the place where living men fight for their living working-class cause. He devotes to work his brain, the brain of a logician, trained in many discussions and syllogisms.

... The man who knocks the ash off his cigar in a smoke-filled room, where balanced judgments dropped from retort-like brains, steps to the window, opens it, and looks out: rubber truncheons swish, street hawkers pull on brown shirts, illegal Communist leaflets scatter. It is time for him to reach solid ground, finally to descend from the cloud-cuckoo-land of logic from which he comes.

He goes on to the street. He speaks not simply poisonous and paradoxical words, fitting only for a rarified intellectual audience; he finds simple words, the simple but powerful truth which can march with heavy feet in the ranks of the proletarians of Wedding, Neukölln, Essen and Hamburg.

Berthold Viertel
Brecht,
Robbed of Citizenship
1938

Oh Brecht, robbed of citizenship. In your leather jacket you now wander in strange cities whose dialects you will never learn, since tongue and soul rise up against this alien gibberish. It is true that you always had something like a dream of emigration, something of Kipling and Gauguin, the longing for the jungle, for Bombay, for the primeval forest, for fabled India and wise China. The heart of a colonialist rumbles within you, the romanticism of boyhood and running away never left your poetic blood. But what actually happened was not what was intended.

They have not been able to make you an emigrant; you have demonstrated that yourself here, with some verses which were moving through the force of their words, verses which have been a distinction for us. You refuse to be a German emigrant, but solely a person driven out, a hunted person, whose thoughts, feelings and plans circle restlessly round German soil, the German people, whose future will be your future despite their alienated present. Until then: need, want and struggle. That is the way I met you in the London fog: above the leather jacket and under the English cap the most German of faces, the head of Schiller, but sharpened, pitted by storm and weather.

You, Brecht, are a lively fighting cock. But your face: Dürer might have designed it, a little less modern; Holbein could have painted it. But you can find it also in Brueghel the peasant. This face could be that of a peasant from the other wars of liberation, which were bloody and fruitless. There is so much Reformation in it, bones, strength, and tense defiance. All that exists in Germany of defiance, sober idealism and desire for accomplished reality is expressed in your frank face. Even Wedekind, that cynically reversed Schiller, seems like an actor compared to you. For your face is that of a non-actor, bony, unpainted, honest, a naked and true face. It is so German that one could laugh and cry at it. It is as German as Hitler's is un-German. But still they stole the citizenship of one, and granted citizenship to the other. The two photographs alone, offered as a choice, without caption, are a placard of the alienation which has taken place there.

In other periods you would have become a Bohemian, or a new Villon with South-German temperament, a cynic with the lute, or even a troubadour, a Walther von der Vogel-weide, a bringer of renewal to folk song — yes, but in which period? The poet is powerful in Brecht. There are fine and beautiful verses in his *Household Homilies*, which are also so biting, and which every German should possess together with his bitter and his sweet pills. What simpleness and directness of magic! What originality in the age of the imitators. In *Baal*, his youthful play, there is such an outbreak of luxuriating pantheism, such a treasure of romantic and over-romantic nature. From this material the Creator could have made ten poets.

But there was a break in the gifted exuberance of emotions, the great hymn to the joys of living, which opened up with such an almost tropical and closely growing richness of colours and tones. This spring night brought frost. An inversion occurred. With his *Drums in the Night* Brecht came marching home from the wars. This was a different homecomer, a different drummer from the man who finally sounded the false reveille. Revolt, the re-evaluation of all patriotic values appeared with compelling, staggering effect, with destructive strength, in the *Ballad of the Soldier*. Brecht learned anew. He had allowed his dialectical materialism to go sour without realising that in its stead a few blown-up phrases were sufficient, both in home and foreign policy — for the time being. Brecht's new thought was materialist:

and what thought! Thought, let alone materialist thought, is not the right diet for all writers, particularly if they have to learn it first. The danger is that emotion gets lost in thought and cannot find the way out — except the exit to the practical. Brecht prevailed. He went the whole way, radically, and did not spare himself.

I was present when he, the most original of all our directors, re-wrote *Baal* for its first staging. The romantic was expunged and replaced by the social; jungle literature was converted into city literature, asphalt literature. This was done at top speed, under inner compulsion, but with the most daring and the shortest outlook towards the sharpest reality. The audience, the still bourgeois audience, could not make much of it. The audience only really warmed up to *The Threepenny Opera,* happily applauding the daring travesty, the pseudo-romantic idealisation of the lumpen-proletariat, and the resultant magical interchange between deep derision and sensuous anarchy. They did not understand that it was their necks which were threatened if they did not, for themselves, make the decision which lurked behind the catchy songs. Egged on by Brecht, a libertine Musagetes, they danced happily on the brown precipice.

But Brecht, unspoilt by success (and here I salute him), wrote *Saint Joan of the Stockyards,* a modern political drama in Shakespearian blank verse, which he sharpened to a fine edge. The bloody humour of the situation was that here stock-exchange manipulation attained a Shakespearian scale. But this Saint Joan really was the people, questioning and searching, and finally taking the decision for a general strike. This play, the most daring and grandiose dramatic work since the war, the most important experiment of the generation, could not be staged. Instead they put on Germany's Awakening. ["Germany awake" — Nazi slogan, trans.] Before this occurred, Brecht — describing in advance everything that happened later and will still happen — wrote *The Round-Heads and the Pointed-Heads,* possibly the only political comedy of the Germans which contains considerable thought. Compared to this play, "The Beaver Coat" despite all its humorous plenitude of life is simply a middle-class idyll. *Round-Heads,* which borrows the outline of its basic plot from Shakespeare's "Measure for Measure", tells how Hitler is appointed by Hindenburg, how the fox is set to watch the geese, and what happens then.

The social penetration of thought is just as consistent as its pictorial presentation and allegorisation of politico-economic conflicts is rich and fruitful. This play, with Hanns Eisler's music for the scattered topical verses, should be translated into English and shown in Britain and America, since it is banished from the country which most urgently needs its poets and scholars. But oh, he has been deprived of his citizenship, he has been withdrawn from that portion of humanity which created him as a vital organ.

Arnold Zweig
Brecht Summary

1934

I.

Brecht always appeared to us as the most important poetical force amongst our younger colleagues. From the very beginning we caught the melody which vibrated through his scenes and ballads. We saw him as a descendant of the folk singers, the unknown poets of the open road, of Georg Büchner and the young romanticism of Brentano and Arnim, and finally of Wedekind.

Then he fell victim to the magic of the fantasy, the intoxication, which emanated from reports on America, and to that melody in Kipling's Indian stories which characteristically enough has escaped the ear of those who translated Kipling's collected works into German.

Brecht set about reviving German theatre, with great talent, ready for a fight, very nonchalant, at a time when it was staggering from expressionist desolation to "contemporary-drama" desolation and ever deeper. He awakened the displeasure of all philistines, including those appearing modern, including the young critics, who did not grasp that Chicago and the Indians were only a matter of style for the Augsburg poet — bridges which located, in alien and far-distant lands, those forces of the soul and those explosive issues of the times which could only be treated thus.

Brecht the balladeer always utilised emotional reality, but in this way he avoided the barbarous naturalism of the Hauptmann imitators, and at the same time attracted the fury of those who could only understand such naturalism. The transformation of Galy Gay in *Man is Man*, and the philosophical conviction of the unessentiality of individualism which inspired it, could only be made believable if transported to India: simultaneously an enchanting game and genuine entity formation.

The entanglement of a host of whites in the motionless and incomprehensible influence of the Malayan Shlink was only possible in that fantastic Chicago which the inexorable fantasy of Brecht the compulsive reader distilled from multiple reports.

We recall these plays, including the *Edward* written together with Feuchtwanger, and also *Baal*, and *Drums in the Night* since they were once German reality, wonderful achievements of German theatre, not least as a result of the great talents as a director of Brecht the writer.

The Kammerspiele in Munich and Berlin, the Deutsches Theater, the Staatstheater were all privileged to present on their stages that high standard established by the settings of Caspar Neher and maintained until the final syllable by Helene Weigel, Koppenhöfer, Homolka and Kortner ...

2.

Then, in his first big success, Brecht took the public by the collar and pulled it along, in *The Threepenny Opera* and in the naked and honest criminal atmosphere of the enticing city of *Mahagonny*. Brecht the poet, in the course of an intellectual transformation, had allowed himself to pull the skin off modern society, and to disclose what lay beneath. He did this by means of figures, songs which were stamped rhythmically on the whole world by Kurt Weill's music; he created figures which only came to full flower in the simple straightforwardness of the Third Reich. Originally it appeared to be a really Brechtian exaggeration to make a criminal the Chief of Police, or to have somebody executed by the decision of a court consisting entirely of his opponents; but in the Third Reich this was far outdone. All of Brecht's bandits are only a pale prediction of the unforgettable types which parade today as the pick of the Third Reich. Ever and again we see that poetic fantasy, as soon as its figures are a few years old, must blush at the way in which reality has copied its figures. This does not rob them of their buffoonish gruesomeness, their fairy-tale reality and the striking power of their verse.

But the real poet Brecht was mainly visible during that period in a number of thin grey volumes. He called them *Experiments* and to make them he exploited certain assistants, whom he unsuccessfully attempted to tear from their anonymity by naming their names. In this way there came into existence "didactic plays", scenes, anecdotes, an excellent children's book *The Three Soldiers*, the umpteenth version of *Saint Joan of the Stockyards*, a Shakespeare adaptation, *The Round-Heads and the Pointed-Heads* which I unfortunately do not know, a number of essays, and above all poems — poems born from the spirit of antiquity in the spirit of modern prose, creating something absolutely new: an antique simplicity never attained by either Rilke or George, coupled with the most direct link with real life — poems of our times, essential, stirring us and enticing us. And amongst them are poems which, recited naturally, could be understood by every worker, every typist tired from the office.

It is useful to examine with a magnifying glass the reality content of some of George's famous poems, to demand from them the truth value which we can expect from every page of Tolstoy, from every anecdote written by Johann Peter Hebel; this may differ in kind but not in reality content from a prosaic report of a boat trip in the mist or the shape of a stone-pine blown by the sea wind. If you do this you will grasp the degree of moral freshness of Brecht's poems — all of them. George has one single determinant experience, that of man in the landscape. Only in this is he genuine, forceful, great and fine. Everywhere else we find the world view and the reality content of a small Catholic philologist, with pompous ideas derived from a world of paper and plaster antiquities.

And while George always squints grotesquely to see

whether he is pumping up an angel or an emperor, Brecht is writing verses which are thoroughly of today, but which could figure in any Roman inscription, verses which make important parts of our life, of our times accessible. By stating them he makes them comprehensible and do-able for everybody — including those who were already capable of doing them but not of feeling the inner impulse which lay in the deed.

3.

There are thirty-three poems in the small volume *Songs, Poems, Choruses* with music by Hanns Eisler published by Editions du Carrefour, Paris, which is a lasting memorial to German verse. Apart from the works of Heinrich Heine there is probably, in this literature so poor in conviction, no other work which is so entirely imbued with a certain attitude toward the world, and this a fighting attitude.

It is an immediate temptation to grasp these verses, both short and long, from the breath of conviction which filled them when Brecht was honing them. They stand there light-footed, at the same time irremovable from the form which they have been given, the most earnest work of a really creative man who seeks nothing except the most precise expression of his militant conviction, and thereby gives birth to the melody which fits and relates these poems so well to our feelings and our intellectual life. Here it becomes plain once again that the form is determined by the spirit; that the poetic mood arises from the wild attack of the objective impulse; that the interchange of line and interval is governed by pathos in everyday dress; that an important part of a sentence is emphasised by the sentence which follows.

The mysterious laws are nowhere infringed — those laws of interaction, of intercrossing and syncopation with which in the fields of poetry the inner sense and grammatical sentence-formation play one against the other; and nowhere do we hear such enchanting secret music as in these verses,

87

for instance those from *The Mother* and *The Measures Taken,* or *The Vanished Fame of the Great City of New York* or the *Song of a Poet.* The intellectual work which Brecht has undertaken in the past five years, in which he developed irresistibly from ballad poet and theatre writer to convinced Marxist socialist, has brought him to a new art, since he is a poet of primitive strength, and his fantasy penetrates in those spheres in which weaker writers are simply flat and tinny.

If you read the *Report on the Death of a Comrade* line by line, you will note how the objects mentioned become transparent: the wall, the rifles, the bullets, chains, chimneys; behind them emerge the essentially similar people whose hands made them, and who differ only in detail from the "I" of the poem who is to be shot; the only essential difference is the level of consciousness which they possess. In the simplest tone of voice Brecht creates this transparence, thus developing a real display of intrinsic values which is far superior to the passive display of values in the works of Rilke and Hofmannsthal, let alone the minor figures amongst the melody-makers. These poems by Brecht can be used like tools, and they base themselves upon the fact that the world is in motion, and can be changed by men and women, either individually or in the mass. And they have too the beauty of tools but (since they are works of art and held at a suitable distance from the real words of the day) the beauty of tools taken from a grave, so that their function in daily life has been suspended by a long span of time and the simplicity of the needs which they once met. But they are reconstructed cleanly of the conversational content of today; there is no word in them which every one of us has not once used, but every word stands as if newborn in the combination of lines, verses and poems. Brecht's very first book of poems, the *Household Homilies,* contained incomparably beautiful creations. But as his latest volume proves the poet has grown into a man; this book has classical stature as testimony of our epoch.

Ruth Berlau
My First Collaboration with Brecht
1960

Meeting in Denmark

I translate *The Mother*. In Denmark Bertolt Brecht was scarcely known, and that only for his *Threepenny Opera*. This was something new — to describe the class struggle in such simple language and with such beauty.

Believe me, it was not easy to translate. This affected not simply me. Brecht's translators all over the world suffer as I suffered then, bearing the great responsibility of translating his language.

For the poems I got the greatest Danish poet; but he was too lyrical, too energetic, and there were battles about every verse; the difficulty was increased by the fact that the verses had to fit Hanns Eisler's music.

I had confessed in a letter what I had stolen; now I wrote again and complained of my difficulties. Brecht replied: "That will change during the rehearsals, just get on with the practical work. You will see that your workers will change things themselves. Can the Mother sing?"

The Danish Mother was a working woman, who scrubbed the steps at a big railway station before coming to rehearsals. There were workers from all sorts of jobs; but many were unemployed, and they looked even more exhausted from their continual walking about searching for work than those who had toiled all day for the exploiters. Many came because they enjoyed making theatre, others because word had got around that it was warm and there was coffee and sandwiches at my place. There were few Communists present when we started rehearsals, and many when we had finished our work. That is what happens when you deal with the works of Bertolt Brecht: his militant art wins not only the audience for our cause, but also the actors. Many from this group fought in Spain. Four were buried in Spain's red earth, but those who returned related how the International Brigades sung Brecht's songs of struggle in twenty-seven different languages as they fought against Franco's hordes before Madrid.

The Rehearsals

I had previously staged many plays with workers. The first had been a play written by sailors themselves. But I had never seen such attention — weariness vanished, and we could keep going much longer. But I became uncertain, or rather certain that I was doing things wrong; I did not know the new way since I had been trained in the traditional Royal Theatre and still acted there.

Then I made the five-hour trip to Svendborg and collected Brecht. For the evening I had rented a cellar. The rehearsals had progressed so far that we needed more room, and obviously the projection apparatus would have to work.

But it did not work, and unfortunately this was not the only thing which did not function.

Everybody had been pleased by the idea of meeting the writer himself, and set about things as never before; everything which had been decided beforehand was forgotten in the effort of producing something for the author.

Brecht stood in a corner with his famous cigar and his comfortable cap.

And there, in that cellar, I first heard him laugh. He laughed loudly a number of times, and pointed at one of those who had come to make theatre.

I went to his corner, and he whispered: "It is comical when workers want to play actors," and added, "and tragic when actors can't play workers."

Suddenly I understood that everything was wrong.

So we started right from the beginning. Brecht knew no

Danish, but he acted to them what he wanted. They imitated him, and it soon became plain that when the gestures, movements, action and groupings were correct, the responses came better. The workers immediately understood and laughed themselves when someone slipped again into the wrong tone; finally we had reached the stage where the one who had made the mistake himself laughed. Then Brecht shouted: "Fine, because somebody who can laugh at himself is already half a god. God laughs all day long at himself."

But then he went home and cursed us in his poem *Speech to Danish Worker-Actors on the Art of Observation.* No sort of work was lost time for Brecht: he could always use everything in one way or another. I would beg you to read this poem patiently, read it twice.

Why? It is so long, you will say.

And I say to you: I started to write this book about Bertolt Brecht half a year before he died. I always showed him what I had written and he gave me advice: "That is conventional and novel-like, you must describe things more . . ."

And another time he said: "Poems are so difficult to read, particularly for young people, workers; if you should find a chance to work it in, explain why I wrote about this or that, and it will be more easily understood . . ." He wanted to be understood by our new readers, by those who could not even know his name, since Hitler had burned his books. He wanted to be popularised, used as a weapon of struggle.

That evening down in the cellar something remarkable happened. Brecht might perhaps have said that this sounds conventional and novel-like, but I would like to describe it to you as best I can:

Brecht, who had paid extremely close attention the whole time was suddenly absent-minded. He had turned his head a little and was looking into one corner. I cannot say how long it lasted, but at any rate so long that we began to get uneasy. Gradually other heads began to turn towards this corner. Slowly Brecht turned towards us again, but it was

as though he no longer saw us. He was somewhere far away;
I knew where he was. And then he said: "Let's get on with
it." He had not noticed our amazement, or the quiet tears
of a Jewish woman who had fled from Germany.

The rehearsal continued.

In the corner stood the red flag: he had been with his
compatriots. With his persecuted compatriots, with the red
flag, there where it could no longer be seen, but was still
there — under the earth. Where, on May Day, it still flut-
tered, raised by real heroes risking their lives.

Much later, when he had to flee from Denmark too and
was working in America, I found the following two lines
in a poem:

> *Oh, flag of the workers drama group*
> *In the old city of Köbenhavn!*

He had not forgotten the flag in the corner of the cellar.

I am telling you all this so that you should not regard
everything as quite natural — so that you look at the flag
with other eyes than many of those in that cellar; many
Danes only learnt to love the flag when Hitler also over-
ran Denmark.

Hanns Eisler
Bertolt Brecht and Music
1957

> "Noteworthy are not only the serious acts of great
> and noble men: I believe that what they do in hours
> of recreation and play is also worthy of attention."
>
> Xenophon, "The Feast of Kallias"

1. The Baden Didactic Play

In 1929 Brecht wrote a didactic play for the music festival
in Baden-Baden. The music was written by Paul Hindemith.
It was a great production and wonderful music.

One episode was a clowning scene: after some instructive
discussion on the weakness of human nature, two clowns
saw off the feet of a third clown. These feet were stilts
crudely made of wood. This rough joke appalled many spectators. Some fainted, although only wood was being sawed,
and the performance was certainly not naturalistic. I sat next
to a well-known music critic who fainted. I helped him out
and got him a glass of water.

When I told Brecht this, he said: "That's really silly, the
man wouldn't faint in a symphony concert, though they are
always sawing there — on the violins. (Brecht hated violins.)
I am disappointed."

2. Brecht and Arnold Schönberg

With some hesitation I introduced Brecht to my teacher
Arnold Schönberg. It was in 1942 in Hollywood. There were
two reasons for me to hesitate: I did not want my respected

93

and ailing teacher Arnold Schönberg to be upset by some remark of Brecht's which Brecht could not anticipate; and I also did not want Arnold Schönberg to make one of his stupid remarks against socialism, which I was used to taking in silence, since he was sick and must not be excited. However I could not demand this of Brecht, for Brecht was in this respect loud, sharp and uncompromising; and I did not want Brecht to be loud, sharp and uncompromising to the sick man Schönberg.

Things went better than I expected, though Schönberg had no idea who Brecht was, and Brecht rejected Schönberg's music in a manner which a modern composer will think monstrous: "Schönberg is too melodious for me, too sweet." After an hour's exchange of politenesses, Schönberg related one of his experiences with donkeys. Brecht was delighted, the two had found common ground, Brecht too had experiences with donkeys.

Schönberg related: "Once I climbed a hill, and since I have a weak heart the steep path was very difficult for me. But in front of me there walked a donkey. He did not walk up the steep path, but always in a zigzag left and right of the path, thus compensating for the steepness. So I imitated him, and now I can say that I have learned something from a donkey." Brecht made from this a poem in honour of Arnold Schönberg's seventieth birthday. It will be found among Brecht's papers.

3. Misuc

Brecht's rejection of certain sorts of music was so extreme that he invented another variety of music-making, which he called "misuc". Misuc he regarded as a way of music-making basically differing from music, since it is misuc and not music.

Brecht's efforts in this field were really based upon his dislike of Beethoven's symphonies (though he loved the music of Bach and Mozart). For thirty years I tried to prove to him that Beethoven was a great master. He often admitted as much to me; but after doing so he was ill-tempered and looked at me distrustfully. "His music always reminds one of paintings of battles," he said. By this Brecht meant that Beethoven had fought Napoleon's battles once again on music paper. And since he did not admire the originals — Brecht had not much sympathy for battles — he did not like the imitations either. For this reason, and for other reasons too, he invented what he called misuc.

For a musician it is difficult to describe misuc. Above all it is not decadent and formalist, but extremely close to the people. It recalls, perhaps, the singing of working women in a back courtyard on Sunday afternoons. Brecht's dislike of music ceremoniously produced in large concert halls by painstaking gentlemen in tails also forms a constituent of misuc. In misuc nobody may wear tails and nothing may be ceremonious. I hope I am interpreting Brecht correctly when I add that misuc aims at being a branch of the arts which avoids something frequently produced by symphony concerts and operas — emotional confusion. Brecht was never ready to hand in his brain at the cloakroom. He regarded the use of reason as one of the best recreations.

Brecht's strivings for reason in music are a heavy blow for us musicians. For in the case of music, where is reason? I have friends who would not go through fire in the cause of reason in music.

Writing these lines, I recall that Brecht accused me of having a sceptical and condescending attitude towards misuc, his invention. Unfortunately he was right.

95

Wieland Herzfelde
On Bertolt Brecht
1956

In May 1939, in those tense months which preceded the Second World War, I got into conversation with an English woman on a ship bound for America. She asked me why I was emigrating to America. I said I was not emigrating; as an enemy of Nazism I and my friends were convinced that we would return. I named some names; she knew none of them, not even that of Thomas Mann. Then she asked whether I thought that contemporary German literature was of world importance, like the German classics, of which she obviously knew something. I replied: "Yes!", and quoted as an example a passage from Brecht's *German Marginal Notes*, four lines which I translated as well as I could into English, naturally losing something in the process. The lines go like this:

> *On the wall it said in chalk:*
> *They want war.*
> *He who wrote it*
> *Is already fallen.*

The effect was very surprising for me. The young woman was suddenly convinced that danger for humanity was approaching, and this conviction was so deep that she went round the whole ship, quoting Brecht's lines as proof of the seriousness of the danger of war.

I mention this incident since it appears to me to illustrate what it is about Brecht that makes such a deep impression: what he says has a message for everyone. In his case literature is not simply aimed at those with literary interests, though the strength of his formulations and the exactitude and vivid pictures of his language make even his shortest utterance a matter of literature. This unity in contradiction of the general and the particular are characteristic for Brecht's person.

When I first met Brecht I could not agree with him without further ado. This was the way with many. I got to know him as a very argumentative, very polished, and even sharp-tongued person. He had a passion bordering upon intolerance for saying things which shocked, and did not accept contradiction without protest.

I remember a celebration of the anniversary of the October Revolution in the Soviet Embassy on Unter den Linden shortly after the great success of *The Threepenny Opera*. Brecht in his exceptionally modest grey suit stood there amongst a number of generals of various nationalities, and other gentlemen extremely well dressed in contrast to him. He was engaged in a discussion on the problems of epic theatre. I had seen *The Threepenny Opera* two evenings running. The first time I had been astonished, impressed, but by no means certain of my verdict. The second time it almost seemed as though I was used to such performances. It was only now that the importance of this new style of theatre came home to me; what I could not yet digest were the theoretical notes on the play in the printed programme. I made some remarks to this effect, and Brecht, whom I had previously not met, simply interrupted me: I should attend to my own work; I understood nothing about the theatre. He was quite right; I had spoken as a spectator and reader. The curious thing was that the remark came from a face which had such a winning look that it was attractive instead of forbidding. And in fact a short while later, particularly in the first period of emigration, we began to work together. Earlier I had been able to attend discussions directed by Brecht in MASCH, the Marxist Workers' School. He was not so interested in discussing with fellow writers, critics and other people interested in culture, as in learning of the experiences of revolutionary workers and their reactions to his writings. For me it was a new and thrilling experience to listen to a writer who discussed questions of the theatre, questions of combining theatrical work and revolutionary work, with all the seriousness with which a commission of doctors discusses a difficult diagnosis.

During the period of emigration I had the chance to publish his works. The word "Works" awakened at first his hostility. He called his plays *Experiments*. I held that the time had come when they should be published under another title; on the basis of my experience as a publisher I feared that the title *Experiments* would be understood as something to be confined to experts, like, for instance, technical experiments. I was able to convince him, and in fact two volumes, two thick volumes, of his *Collected Works* were published; two further volumes were almost completed when they fell into the hands of the Nazi troops marching into Czechoslovakia and were destroyed.

We also debated as to whether the initial letters of the nouns should be written in capitals or not [in German, trans.]. At that time there was a principle of using only small letters, as in other languages; I do not know whether this originated with Stefan George, but it was particularly striking in his case. I regarded this as yet another method of keeping literature away from the readers. It was not easy to convince Brecht; he thought that capital letters were too flatulent. In his letters he kept to this rule: he even generally wrote his name with a small "b". At this point we are faced with the question: Was Brecht modern at all costs? For a long period, particularly before I got to know him, it appeared to me that he tended to write as though he wanted to hit people on the head. Even before Brecht's day this had been regarded as modern. However, I came to see that in Brecht's case the situation was different. When he was still at school he had been hit on the head, and this had given him headaches; now he was doing in his way things which would give other people headaches.

There was a great gap between the people whom he

represented and those who were only a little older than he, or those who as writers clung to the forms and feelings of the older generation. I explain this gap thus: in 1914 there were young people for whom youth suddenly stopped when they were sent to the front. They lay at the front with doleful memories of their lost pre-war youth. But those who were only one year or a couple of years younger continued to go to school or to learn a trade; they did not experience the sudden change in the times as a headlong descent, and did not yearn for their youth as a part of those old times. Ilya Ehrenburg said once that it was the tragedy of his generation to stand with one foot in the nineteenth century and the other foot in the twentieth century. That is what I mean. Ehrenburg's generation, and mine too, stood a little in the previous century. Brecht, on the other hand, like Anna Seghers, stood completely in this century. As a result he completely lacked certain characteristics of the older generation.

However, he had two qualities which always struck me as extremely young, and which astonished me and made me almost envious; he was completely unsentimental, and never looked back regretfully to the past. For him the "old times" did not exist; there was simply an unreasonable, unjust, vicious and warlike world which had to be changed. He did not say, like Leonhard Frank: "The world is good," but rather:

> Make sure when leaving the world
> Not just that you were good, but leave
> A good world.

It is not surprising that the young Brecht encountered that doctrine which demands that the world should be changed. He understood Marxism in a particularly wide and deep sense, as something demanding the whole person and all his deeds; not simply as a programme for political thought and political deed, but a programme for thought and deed as a whole. Brecht's style, his way of observing and writing, were governed by the recognition that every development proceeds dialectically. He not only perceived the contradictory nature of events, but tried to uncover the social roots of the contradictions, and to examine what they revealed.

Here are two examples: in a circle of politically aware people, there was a discussion as to which country was more modern, Germany or the United States. No agreement could be reached. Then Brecht joined them, and he was selected as umpire. Without hesitation he said that America was more modern, giving the following reason: if Germany continues to develop on a capitalist basis, it will take it decades to achieve the low point already reached by America. On another occasion he claimed, to the astonishment of his hearers, that the best soldiers in the world were the Russians and the Italians. This was at the time of the Italian defeats in Albania. Asked why he had picked the Italians, who ran away at every opportunity, he replied that they knew for whom and for what they had been sent into battle. For him the best soldiers were soldiers who think.

Brecht, the writer full of fantasy, the good fighter, was a teacher and educator. The main principle of this educational work was the rejection of phrasiness and of decoration for decoration's sake. He too could not fill his stomach with words. He wanted clarity, and he knew that clarity could not be attained by declamation. When he made statements without giving the proofs, he did this with the provocative intention of challenging people to search for the reasons. His theoretical terminology, for instance in his essays *On Rhymeless Verse with Irregular Rhythm, Small Organon for the Theatre* and the notes to his plays, was in part created by himself; this had to be so since he had things to say for which there was no literary vocabulary. This resulted in a number of misunderstandings.

In his literary work on the other hand, the figurative element is decisive, and it is the configuration which makes it possible for the non-expert, for people not concerned with literature and the theatre, to follow him; and they can sometimes do it better than the professionals. It was characteristic of Brecht to make complicated matters simpler by use of a picture, and this was shown by one of his earliest poems, the *Legend of the Dead Soldier*. This includes the lines:

> *You could, if you wore no helmet,*
> *See the stars of home.*

Helmets in general, and the German steel helmets of the First World War in particular, have the peculiarity that they block the outlook upward. When Brecht says that you could "see the stars of home" he includes the small reservation "if you wore no helmet," making it clear that the stars of home are invisible to people incapable of seeing over the brim of their helmets. Brecht therefore had already said back in 1918 what he said again and again in other words and with other illustrations until a short time ago.

Various incorrect things have been said about Brecht. He is supposed to have had an inclination towards anarchism before he dramatised Gorky's "Mother". In reality he always had a very strong feeling for revolutionary authority. One of his early plans was to give poetic form to the Communist Manifesto. In the *United Front Song* there is an example:

> *The emancipation of the working class*
> *Is a matter for the workers alone.*

His language, lacking everything baroque or laboured, marks Brecht's strict and constructive will, and his maintenance of proportion between feeling and thought as the basis for the grace, humour and lightness of his verse. In the *Children's Hymn* Brecht states:

> *Spare not grace and not endeavour,*
> *Neither passion nor the mind.*

He coupled things which belong in the realm of feelings and the aesthetic, grace and passion, with such different things as endeavour and mind. I believe there was scarcely another poet who so consistently and so consciously emphasised in his poems the connection between thought and feelings, which always exists in reality. His writing, his character and his mode of life are characterised by the co-existence of the easy and the difficult, the serious and the cheerful. He was never surrounded by a stuffy or dejected atmosphere, either at home or at theatre rehearsals; there was always the atmosphere of an obligation to produce something, not to waste time. The same was true of discussion. He liked it very much, and his aim was always not simply to collect impressions and opinions, but to draw conclusions for future behaviour, for further and if possible joint activity.

Brecht had a very high opinion of expertise. He was grateful for serious and concrete criticism, and attached great importance to it. He did not regard anything that he had created as final and complete. His publishers had a hard time with him. Right until the work was printed he altered and supplemented. Like his figure Galileo he tried to make what is new visible in a new manner. It was for this reason that he called his works *Experiments*.

People who had anything to do with him began to change astonishingly quickly. He radiated the obligation to thought-out truth and to concentration on the essentials, and dominated those around him. Naturally weaknesses showed up in a bright light of this sort; and in this sense, as Karl Kleinschmidt wrote in his obituary notice, Brecht was a disturbing person. Brecht did not live all too comfortably either. He could not be indolent, and he could not bear indolence in others either. There was nothing about him which could be described as "comfortable". But he certainly did have all the more heart — though he would never have used the word I have used to describe it. He was concerned about all those he was fond of, who worked with him. He never tired of defending them, standing by them. He was not yielding or soft; in fact he could be merciless when it was a case of preventing the disturbance or misinterpretation of valuable activity. However receptive and helpful

Brecht was, he was not one to complain or even to listen to complaints. He preferred to intervene quickly, energetically and with his entire authority when there was a serious grievance. It was easier to go to him than to any other friend if you were depressed. Simply a look at his clever, unlachrymose, attentive face was sufficient to make you confident. I believe that this is what made him able to do so much. He attracted people, and with him they forgot their small or large personal worries; one of the reasons was that with him they found work waiting, which he let them take part in before they had fully realised it. He won people as his friends by making them his assistants. The names of assistants are to be found in many of his books. Vice versa, Brecht also sometimes became the assistant of his friends. He was very interested in the activities of other people, and spent many hours giving a hand with their work.

Though Brecht was fully occupied or over-occupied as writer and director, and as a steadfast combatant in the political arguments and struggles of the decades which he lived through, he still found the strength to be a friend upon whom you could depend, though he claimed the contrary in the *Ballad of Poor B. B.*

Like all artists, Brecht was receptive to beauty. In his earlier years he emphasised sparseness and utility, but finally he had in his apartment some beautiful old pieces of furniture, some modern drawings, stage designs for his plays, interesting posters, and exotic works of art, particularly Chinese.

When he intervened in the Barlach discussion in the Academy of Arts he said to me: "Who would have thought that I, who always cursed at 'ar-rt', should find myself defending art."

He had a very personal idea of beauty. When he called something beautiful he meant the word in a very broad sense, including the conception that the object was *right*. People whom you would immediately describe as ugly he could find beautiful if they carried out an activity in nearly classical perfection. For Brecht it was an aesthetic pleasure to observe a sack-carrier if it could be said that he displayed the way a sack ought to be carried. He regarded it as beautiful if an act was shown absolutely in its own way through attitude and gesture. One of the secrets of his writing and his work as director was that he could make reality visible in such a special manner, so that it was more impressive and unforgettable than when seen in everyday life.

In addition, you could admire the way in which Brecht met the pressure of obligations which he had laid upon himself. I can only suggest that he thought very little — perhaps too little — of himself. There can scarcely be another writer in whose works the word "I" occurs so seldom, and in which there is so little reference to personal things. It was part of his nature and of his unusual talent that he did not spend so much time on facts as on the question: What is to be done? He defined it himself:

> *Real progress*
> *Is not to have progressed*
> *But progression.*
> *Real progress is*
> *What makes progression possible*
> *Or enforces it.*

When we use the phrase about the "new man" and feel the need to picture a real man, we may think of Brecht. He was a new, a real man.

Max Frisch
Diary, 1948

Brecht

My association with Brecht, exhausting as associating with
somebody of superior intellect probably always is, lasted for
only half a year; the temptation simply to avoid such an
association is sometimes quite considerable. It is then Brecht
who rings up or asks you in the street, always friendly in his
dry and rather controlled fashion, whether you have a free
evening. Brecht looks for discussion as a matter of course.
For my part I get the least from those conversations where
Brecht checkmates me with his dialectic: you are beaten, but
not convinced.

Thinking over his arguments on the way home at night,
I sometimes lose myself in an indignant monologue: that is
all not true! But when I hear similar and often spiteful
remarks, dropped casually by third persons, then I find myself forced to cycle again to Herrliberg.

The simple curiosity which one may feel about someone
famous would, in the long run, scarcely suffice to make one
accept the exertions of such evenings, which always develop
into a confrontation with one's own limitations. Brecht always exerts a fascination, and I ascribe this to the fact that
in his case a life is being lived on the basis of thought. (Our
thoughts are generally only a belated justification; they do
not steer, they are pulled.)

Confronted with overwhelming talent, which Brecht incidentally has, at the moment probably the greatest talent
in the German language, you can defend yourself through
admiration; you kneel like a ministrant at the altar, the
matter rests where it is, and you go away. Confronted with
an attitude this no longer suffices, and quite different chal-

lenges are presented, just because Brecht is less vain about his person than almost anyone, challenges which cannot be met by fawning. Brecht, like perhaps all with an independent attitude towards life, does not expect agreement. On the contrary he expects to be contradicted, he is displeased if the contradiction is cheap, and bored if there is none.

His face, strict, with peasant calm, sometimes masked with craftiness, but always wide-awake, shows that he always listens; even if he regards it as chatter he forces himself to listen. But behind his small hidden eyes the blaze of contradiction plays; his glance flares, impatience makes him first embarrassed and then aggressive, stormy. His flashes of lightning, his remarks, are meant as a challenge which should lead to a real discussion, to an explosion, an argument, but their sharpness sometimes slays. His partners, particularly if they are new and not used to him, fall silent with an uneasy smile. All that Brecht can do then is to control himself and to cathechise them, seriously, somewhat mechanically, basically annoyed since this is the opposite of the conversation which he had hoped for, annoyed too that so few people have really gone through the school of Marxism, Hegelian dialectic, historical materialism.

Brecht does not want to be a lecturer, but he finds himself in the position of a man who wants to talk about poetry, and so that it should not end in chatter the conversation ends with a lesson in elementary grammar, for which the time is in fact too valuable. Despite this he gives the lesson, since mere chatter would be even more annoying; instruction is at least instruction, useful at least for the other person, perhaps useful. But I believe that Brecht is really happy for his part when he does not have to cathechise. Our conversations always become fruitful when I leave the reflections to him, and for my part only supply the hard facts, though these always have the character of contradiction. His attitude — and with Brecht it is really an attitude which incorporates every aspect of life — is the daily application of those results of cogitation which depict our social environment as outstripped, as nefarious in its forcible continuation, so that this society can be regarded solely as an obstacle, not as a yardstick. Brecht is reserved about the future: that will produce something enraging, the danger of immobility for a period which will allow of no further development.

In this connection it is no coincidence that Brecht, in his work with actors, always tries so hard to make them relaxed, not muscle-bound. His own work, where it is poetic, always has this feature to a high degree. Relaxation, ease, these are extraordinary demands in a life such as Brecht lives, a life aimed at a world which has been sketched but which at present exists nowhere; it is visible only in his attitude, which is that of living and unsparing contradiction, never tamed by the hardships of decades of living as an off-sider. Christians have an attitude to the Hereafter, Brecht to the Here-and-now. This is one of the differences between him and the priests, to whom he has a certain resemblance, though he likes to make fun of them on the basis of their differing goals; the doctrine of the end which justifies the means produces resemblances, though the ends are different. There are Jesuits of the Here-and-now too, and sometimes it is not their desire, their supreme obligation, to be understood, or not under all circumstances. *Five Difficulties in Writing the Truth*, a short essay written in 1934 for illegal distribution in the Nazi Reich, has as the title for its fourth paragraph: "The decision to select those in whose hands the truth is effective." And the fifth paragraph is entitled: "The cunning to spread the truth amongst many." One has to recall this, particularly if a larger and accidental group is assembled.

To plan a peaceful and more just world and to stand in front of the guns and be a victim is the attitude to the Hereafter, the heroic; it is not the attitude to the Here-and-now, the practical, the necessary.

Yesterday we went bathing, the first time I had seen Brecht amidst nature, an environment which cannot be changed and is therefore of little interest for him. (*And I saw nature without patience, and so passed the time which was given to me on earth.*) That which must be changed is so great that no time remains to praise that which is natural. Here and in some other ways Brecht is certainly living a gesture; it has become second nature, natural, when he says not a word about nature. He worries only whether we shall get caught in the threatening storm or not. The lake is green, ploughed by the wind, the skies are violet and sulphur yellow. Brecht, wearing as always his grey flat cap, leans on the rather decaying rail and smokes a cigar; it is the decay which he notes; he makes a joke about capitalism. Only when I have started to swim does he go into the hut. There is lightning over the town, slanting rain hangs over the far-off hills, the birds swoop, the leaves of the great beeches rustle, on the road the dust whirls. Later I see Brecht get into the water, swim a few strokes, and soon disappear into the hut, while his wife and I go on swimming in the wind-ruffled water. As I get out Brecht is already clothed again in his grey jacket and grey cap, rendering praise for his refreshment by lighting the next cigar.

"You know," he says in a tone as though we had only paused for an instant, "that seems to me just the thing. The actor who plays Puntila must certainly not create the impression that —"

The flat which Brecht has obtained in Herrliberg is on the top floor of an old gardener's house. We eat in the kitchen, where his wife shows one of her less known talents, or in the hall, which has something attic-like, as has the whole dwelling, something excitingly provisional. Later we stroll on a gravelled roof path, ducking under the washing posts, and finally for coffee we sit down in his study, with a fine window over the lake and the Alps, which Brecht does not notice; he likes the window too, because it gives light. The room is something like a workroom: typewriter, sheets, scissors, crates of books, on one chair lie the newspapers, Swiss, English, German, American; now and then something is cut out and put in a file. On the big table I see glue and brushes, photos, sets from a New York production, Brecht speaks of Laughton. Then there are books being used for the work in progress, the correspondence of Goethe and Schiller, Brecht reads out something dealing with the dramatic and the epic. In addition there is a radio, a packet of cigars, chairs which only allow you to sit upright, I put my ashtray on the firwood floor, on the opposite wall there hangs a Chinese painting which can be rolled up but is now unrolled. Everything is so arranged that you could leave within forty-eight hours; unhomelike. It did not look very different, I think, in Finland in 1941:

> *From the loudspeakers I hear the victory communiqués*
> *of the scum.*
> *Inquisitively I regard the map of the continent.*
> *Right at the top, in Lappland*
> *Towards the northern polar sea*
> *I still see a little door.*

In this connection I realise that Brecht has never spoken of his personal experiences, never said anything about himself, or only very indirectly. We speak about architecture, about dwelling. Brecht walks up and down, sometimes we both stand in order to be able to speak better, walking as though on the stage, and Brecht, reserved though he is, expresses himself strongly in gestures. A small dismissive movement of his hand shows scorn; standing still at the decisive point shows an emergent sentence; a question mark is expressed by a gruff hoisting of the left shoulder; irony is shown by imitating with his bottom lip the confident-homely seriousness of the upright man. His sudden, somewhat rasping, brittle but not cold laugh when an absurdity is taken to an extreme, and then again his engaged and intimidated astonishment, his naked face, when somebody tells him something which really touches, worries or pleases him. Brecht is a fine and friendly man; but conditions are not such that this can suffice.

On my wall hangs a Japanese carving,
Mask of an evil demon, painted with gold enamel.
With sympathy I note
The swollen vein in the brow, showing
How exhausting it is to be evil.

Our relationship prospers best when the conversation, which Brecht always leaves to the ideas and the needs of the others, turns upon theatre questions, of directing, acting, questions of the craft of writing which, soberly considered, inevitably lead to the essentials. Brecht is an untiring discusser. Together with an understanding in art questions which adores scientific methods, he has a childlike gift of questioning. An actor: what is that? What does he do? What special characteristics must he have? A creative patience to start once again from the beginning, to collect experiences, and to question people without forcing the answers upon them. The answers, the first ones, are often of extraordinary meagreness. "An actor," he says hesitantly, "that is probably a person who does something with particular emphasis, for instance drinking or something." His almost peasant-like patience, his courage to stand alone on an empty field, to renounce borrowings, the strength to be quite modest and possibly without result, and then the intelligence to nail down the beginnings of a possible perception, and to allow this to be developed by contradiction, and finally the manliness to take perceptions seriously and act accordingly, disregarding other opinions — these are wonderful lessons, exercises, in which one hour weighs more than a semester. The results, however, belong to him. Our profit is to see the way in which he achieves them.

Then the time has come to go home. Brecht takes his cap and the milk jug, which must be placed in front of the door. Brecht is in a curious way courteous, even-tempered, in a manner which has become a gesture, but which is rare. If I have not got my bicycle he accompanies me to the train, waits till I have got in, waves his hand in a short and almost secretive manner, without taking off his grey cap, which would be without style. Avoiding the people he leaves the platform with quick steps, not long and rather light. His arms swing noticeably little, and he always holds his head a little on one side, with his peaked cap pulled down over his forehead as though he wanted to hide his face, half conspiratorially, half shyly.

He looks, if you see him like this, as unobtrusive as a worker, a metalworker, but too unrobust for a worker; too graceful, too wide-awake for a peasant; altogether too mercurial for somebody from these parts. Hiding and alert, a refugee who has left many stations, too shy for a man of the world, too experienced for a professor, too knowledgeable not to be fearful; a stateless citizen, a man with a limited residence permit, a passer-by of our times, a man named Brecht, a physicist, a poet without adulation . . .

The manuscript he has given me to read is entitled *Small Organon for the Theatre.* Brecht wants to know what I find in it. Our misunderstanding he regards as useful too; it warns him. I have never met anyone who, without making it a pose, is so free of prestige. An actor, not a great one, makes a textual suggestion: he would like to say something at a point where the play ordains silence. Brecht listens, considers, and agrees; not for the sake of giving way, but because the suggestion is right. His rehearsals never have the air of a boudoir, rather that of a workshop. In other ways too Brecht shows this serious readiness, which is not flattery and which tolerates no flattery; he shows the modest impersonality of a wise man, learning through everyone who crosses his path: not from him, but through him.

Letzigraben

With Brecht on the building site. Since he refuses to lift the telephone during working hours, I had to collect him from his desk, in accordance with his instructions. As always, he is ready to do anything which promises to be an objective lesson. From the midst of a scene which he has in the typewriter he puts on his shoes. On the bed lie stage designs for Berlin, sketches which interest me. But he wants to get to the building site; you can talk about theatre in bad weather. Of all those whom I have so far shown around the building site, Brecht is by far the most responsive, eager for knowledge, and expert in questioning. Experts easily forget the big basic questions; amateurs listen, accept answers to questions they would never have asked; particularly unproductive are the literary people, who faced with hard facts retreat into meditation before they understand them; they are creatures of their feelings, whipping the froth of their wit or their inwardness.

Brecht has an astonishing eye, with intelligence as a magnet which attracts the problems, in such a way that they emerge even from behind the existing solutions. To explain to him how a tower came about, how the architectural form developed from the static formulae, and not only how it developed but how the form should not only fulfil its purpose but also explain this purpose to the eye — such explanations become a real pleasure, a shared pleasure. For over two hours we stalk around, upstairs and down, in and out and round. In addition there is with him the factor which inevitably divides the creative person from the expert — the brotherliness, the consciousness arising from the experience: In the beginning there is nothing. The experts, when they see a drawing, examine it against the background of Dürer, Rembrandt or Picasso; the creative person, whatever his field, sees the blank paper.

Günther Weisenborn
Zurich Diary
Note of May 1948

He is standing on the terrace of his house near Zurich, and is the same old Brecht, lean, short and bowed. His Roman hair gleams black-grey, and his black eyes are hidden behind heavy black spectacles. Far across Lake Zurich we see the white Alpine chain looming in the April light, and we discuss tension, alienation effects, epic drama and placeless drama. His arguments are delivered with a precision which betrays long consideration. In all his works there is no description of nature, he says. He reads aloud one of Schiller's letters, one of his ballads, all with that sharp Bavarian voice which betrays his old dialectical love of a fight, the voice which I still have in my ear from earlier days.

A master of intellectual analysis, a hermit between America and Europe who sometimes changes into a Chinese sage; a German classic who has circled the world in fourteen years and is now on the point of returning to Berlin. The cigar is always burning in his outstretched hand. He has remained true to his flat cap, and with the patience of a good teacher he walks through the streets of the town, unpretentious, alien and ironic. In his workroom here there still hangs that Chinese scroll painting of a friendly scholar which we used to unroll in Berlin when there was a pause in work. We recall this, and Brecht laughs with pleasure.

On microfilms he has brought his works with him. They all go into a little box, he says. He is — like Valéry — tuned in to the great mechanism of the world; he is a chemist in his laboratory, in which he develops future forms, a secretive chemist who despises secrecy, and — excuse me, Brecht — a marvellous poet.

Max Schroeder
Brecht's Stage Style
1949

In the 1920s the stage style which Bertolt Brecht created for the presentation of his works — a style which included equally words, music and image — was often regarded as a sectarian experimental style. In front of the bare round background there stand only a few flats when the short curtain which covers the lower half of the stage rises — that curtain which is used between scenes for the projection of written texts. The thinly manned orchestra sits in a box, and acoustically it does not fill the auditorium. The actors perform with controlled gestures, avoiding emphasis and crescendo. Songs are delivered from the footlights, while action comes to a standstill on the stage. The rhythm of the songs is sometimes derived directly from the barrel organ. To eyes and ears accustomed to the technique of illusion of Richard Wagner's stage, Brecht's apparatus appeared spare and austere.

But the productions of *The Threepenny Opera* and the comedy *Man is Man* displayed astonishingly the power of illusion in the apparently sparse means used by Brecht's stage. It became apparent that the economy of instruments, the low volume of the intonation (of words and music), the colours which scarcely emerged from grey, all provided an extremely rich and fine scale of intermediate tones, and an enhancement of means which never reached an extreme. The details impressed themselves readily upon the eye and the ear, so that Brecht's tunes, formulations and images remained in the head, even when the ideas which they embodied were not immediately intelligible to everybody, or even seemed nonsensical.

Many people regarded the nuts presented for the cracking by each Brecht production as mannered buffoonery. People hummed the tunes and quoted the verses, but regarded the exotic and picturesque setting as responsible for the fascination. The same sparse means are responsible for the enormous and intoxicating effect created by the opening scene of *Mother Courage*. We see nothing which we have not been able to see daily for years on country roads — and in the city — and hear a song the words of which are hardly distinguishable, as if blown to us on the wind.

On a covered waggon, pulled by two youths, two peasant-looking women roll across the bare revolving stage. A text is projected stating that the events play in the Thirty Years' War. For the audience this is no leap into the past, but a fairy-tale extension of the present. Never again will we see a covered wagon pulled by human power without recalling this scene and this song. The production has, with its first scene, made an indelible mark on our knowledge, which will continue to work within us.

The economical use of props on Brecht's stage is neither aesthetic trifling nor its opposite, ascetic contempt for art. This economy helps to make the content of the writing transparent and graspable for the spectator. The romantic theatre of illusion, which reached its climax with Richard Wagner, rose to a fortissimo of colour and sound, trying to grasp and transport the spectator emotionally; Brecht, on the other hand, generally confines himself to the tones of conversation. He does not present the spectator continually with the increased emotions which are expected, but forces him actively to acquire these emotions as when reading a clearly printed book.

For the friend of the arts this may be nothing new, since every acquisition of art involves reading and digesting. In the use of his means of presentation Brecht is by no means without tradition. He has adopted stimuli from all sorts of places, ranging from the chapman's ballad to Chinese theatre. He is constantly determined that the spectator should not be lulled by illusions, that the listener should not think that he has understood something when he has actually not understood it (which is the quintessence of decadent romantic theatre — and of modern amusement art). He forces the public to learn to decipher his art, as a progressive form of society teaches its illiterates to read. He fights against the mysticism and superstition spread over the understanding of the arts by decadent bourgeois ideology. In this respect there is no contradiction in tendency between Brecht's theatre and the antique theatre or the theatres of Shakespeare and Goethe. Brecht has given himself the task of preserving, under the new historical conditions, the theatre as a factor which can move society.

Brecht perhaps takes the theatre as art — as art itself — more seriously than it has ever been taken before. He realises that it is only as a social affair that it can really be taken seriously. In antiquity, in Shakespeare's renaissance, in Goethe's time, the theatre was taken seriously in accordance with the highest level of world view achieved at the time; at the same time it was subjected to the religious and idealist philosophical limits of each epoch. Brecht is attempting to bring the theatre to the level of the most inclusive world view produced by the social reality of our times, and to use it in the struggle.

In the 1920s there were many attempts to make reforms in this direction; Brecht differs from them in that he derives his style not primarily from the fashioning of the material but from the attitude of the spectator. His style is therefore not, as is usual, developed from the work alone and from an established tradition of presentation; instead it seeks to determine and to fulfil social needs. The terms which Brecht uses, such as "epic theatre", "didactic play" etc., are not formalist dogmas, but stages of experimentation, aimed not at abolishing the "drama" but rather at producing a new encounter with the audience, a more binding encounter than that of the traditional theatre.

The discussion on this subject is by no means concluded;

the production of *Mother Courage* gives us, after a long interval, finally the opportunity to re-open this discussion in Berlin on the basis of a masterpiece. It may be regarded as a fact that after a genuine Brecht production, every receptive spectator takes home the feeling with him that his eyes have been opened, as when he first deciphered the alphabet, or as if he had himself learned to try out a new art.

For Brecht himself, each production of one of his works is a serious undertaking with some resemblance to a ritual ceremony, not the ceremony of a cult entwined in the irrational and the metaphysical, but rather the propagation of culture and enlightenment necessary for the further existence of humanity. A production of *Galileo* will perhaps make this attitude completely clear; but it is also true for the production of *Mother Courage* and the many previous *Experiments* of the poet in his argument with the romanticism in his own early works.

The artistic validity of the Brechtian style is shown, for instance, by the fact that it tunes the actor to a certain gamut; but instead of restricting his creative force, this, on the contrary, develops it most excellently. Where can we see today on the Berlin stage such a moving performance as Helene Weigel as Mother Courage, presented with such harmonious unconcern? Who can forget the scene in which Angelika Hurwicz, as Dumb Kattrin, is shot down from the roof when she, as a human being, does what the backward peasantry vainly ask God to do — warns the threatened townspeople.

Paul Bildt as the cook and Werner Hinz as the army chaplain present figures of an originality and intensity derived from Jacques Callot's sketchbook, and at the same time create the impression that they had just been standing next to us in the overfilled underground train and argued about a sack of wood or less. Kahler and Teege — both of them, like Angelika Hurwicz, from the "younger generation" — condense in their acting the tragedy of the postwar young people, for whom the bourgeois world can show no honourable way out. Kühne as the recruiting officer, Bienert and Segtrop as sergeant-majors, Weber as the colonel, Grosse as the cornet present, with apparent lack of effort, their best abilities. Renate Keith plays with sharp accents and gestures the role of Yvette, the camp whore, the contrasting figure to Dumb Kattrin. The most disparate elements come together in a composition which forces even the most reluctant spectator to accept the thesis that those who plan a war like the Thirty Years' War profane the people to serve their own purposes and have no place in human society.

Brecht's stage is so very exactly arranged artistically that aesthetes attempt to construct a contradiction between this and "political theatre". But actually it reaches its artistic mastery by reason of the fact that it brings to light political truth, that it devotes all its wisdom to clearing away ruins and to building a society proof against the catastrophe politicians. The dramatist and all his co-workers deserve great thanks for this memorable production. It is time for Berlin to have its own Brecht theatre.

Paul Rilla
Brecht from 1918 to 1950

1951

The volume *One Hundred Poems* by Bertolt Brecht, just published, provides an opportunity to view the development of the poet. The volume stretches from 1918 to 1950, from the *Legend of the Dead Soldier,* written by the twenty-year-old in the last year of the First World War, to the great poem *Training the Millet* written in the fifth year after the Second World War.

The span between these two poems makes it possible to observe the contradictions which had to be solved in Brecht's work before the distorted picture of an age to be sneered at and violently attacked could recede behind the undistorted vision of the joyfully affirmed new reality. On one side there is the ghastly grimace of imperialist war; on the other the happy face of socialist peace. On one hand man as a tool, used for ends alien to nature and hostile to life; on the other, in the Soviet Union, man as the measure of every purpose. There man *inspired by the idea of changing nature* makes it subject to him, in order to place it at the service of the new life (and at the service of the struggle against the forces of destruction).

The Contradiction

The irreconcilable contradiction between the dying old period and the emerging new period is the factor which maintains tension in the entire works of Brecht, whether poetry or theatre, fiction or theory. Brecht came to the fore in the 1920s. Movement had come into the social revolution in Germany, and against this social terror was mobilising increasingly massively and increasingly brutally; behind the bourgeois restoration of the Weimar Republic the frightful face of fascism showed itself. At the start Brecht took the right position in his poetry, which stood in opposition to every camouflaged or open bourgeois lie in life and art. This was still the attitude of *The Threepenny Opera*, the great success of which was a triumph over bourgeois amusement-theatre and its social lies. On the one hand *The Threepenny Opera* had a lasting influence as the breakthrough of theatre for the people; on the other hand its slogans of lumpen-proletarian social opposition lagged behind the positive social language of developments. Brecht soon realised that the new popular nature of the theatre would have to implement the breakthrough of the new content. This new content did not remain in opposition, thus subjecting itself to certain conditions of the bourgeois counter-world which it fought; instead it took up new positions, subjecting itself to the conditions of the socialist world to be won.

That Worthy of Mention

In *One Hundred Poems* it is also possible to watch the process by which the negation of inhumane late-bourgeois civilisation develops with increasing consciousness into a positive stand. Brecht's early poems emotionally feel social disorder as a darkening, as something cold. However, these dark times appear to be an adventure, which man can face armed with nothing but the cynicism of his own coldness. Once the adventure has passed, there remains nothing. Nothing except the mockery that this lightweight race, which built such giant buildings, possesses nothing lasting. In 1921 he wrote:

> *And there we sat, a race of lightweights,*
> *In houses said to be indestructable.*

And from 1921 too dates a prophesy terrifying today in its calm tone of statement:

> *From this town there will remain:*
> *What went through it — the wind.*

Brecht had foreseen the perfection of imperialist destruction. The same poem states:

> *And after, there will come:*
> *Nothing worthy of mention.*

But the later poems by Brecht know that something worthy of mention is precisely what is coming; it is not worthy of mention because it comes *after* us, but because it comes *through* us.

The later poems fill the dark times with real facts which define the social position. Things which are only hinted at in the 1921 poem are enlarged in the 1929 work *The Vanished Fame of the Great City of New York* into a grotesque vision, which no longer extends fantasy from empty life into emptiness, but which depicts a real event, the world crisis of monopoly capitalism, the hellish fall of stocks and shares, and gives a prophetic picture of the fall of American mammoth civilisation. This poem does not speak in general about the unfriendliness of the world; it speaks very specifically about the "miserable mistakes" of a social system, and it is this which makes the testimony generally applicable and valid. It attacks the painted megalomania of a barbarous civilisation-enterprise, but not the works of man. Nothing man builds can be too high; but man must build on firm foundations.

In the volume of poems Brecht's farewell to America is followed by the report *The Moscow Workers Take Over the Great Metro on April 27th 1935*. Here too something is being built, this report tells us, but here there are no "miserable mistakes" in the calculations; the sums have been done right. This is a grandiose work of civilisation, not built upon the shifting sandy foundation of social disorder, but upon the mother earth of the socialist community. Here the calculations are correct.

121

And when the line was completed from the best plans,
And the owners came to inspect it, and
To take a ride, then they were those
Who had built it.

The poem reports on the fame of the wonderful work of construction, which in those days saw something never seen by any of its predecessors in many cities and many ages — the building workers as the owners. The poem asks, and needs no reply:

Where had it ever happened before that the fruit of the
work
Had fallen to those who had done the work? And where
Were those who had built it
Not driven from the building?

And daringly and very truly the concluding lines of the poem link this work of socialist humanism with the humanist heritage:

When we saw them riding in their carriages,
The work of their hands, we knew
That this was the fine scene which the great teachers
Once foresaw with awe.

That is how Brecht describes, with the strongest and simplest words, that worthy of mention which had come into the world. But in his book of poems he exercises the right of the chronicler not to omit the contradictions which hindered the words, since they were of that age. And when he asks for the tolerance of *Those Born Later*, recalling the memories of the dark times, then this tolerance is not needed for the poet, who has shown in this book very thoroughly of what man is capable. This thought too is a power, serving the new life. The dark times do not remain dark, for slanting through them comes the light in which the flag flies high: *A wonderful flag and it was red.* And the despair, *If there is only injustice there,* reverses itself in the *Song of the Class Enemy* to a rhythm of rebellion so irresistible that it must be able to part the muddy fascist flood of concentrated injustice.

Praise of the Dialectic

> *The word will never be found,*
> *That can unite us two.*
> *Rain falls from the sky to the ground.*
> *My class enemy is you.*

Brecht's commitment to the struggle of the working class is the result of a consciousness which uses the weapon of the materialist dialectic as a weapon of poetry. Brecht's works contain not simply struggle, but lessons on how to struggle; this is true both of his plays and of his poems. The same poetic language which calculates the facts also calculates their truth or untruth. If the fight is to be rightly waged, then the fighting slogans must be tested. The new and the great feature of Brecht's poems is that they translate clearly into an emotional language this process of testing, of case-hardening the meaning, just as they subject the emotional language of reality to the dialectical test. Brecht's realism is the result of a tension in which one feature challenges the other, in which thought becomes belief, and belief thought.

When the cruelty of fascism descended upon Germany and appeared to block every prospect, Brecht wrote in 1934 the poem *Praise of the Dialectic* in which the language of facts encountered its dialectical counterpart. Force stated: *As things are, so shall they remain.* And amongst the oppressed many say: *What we want will never be.* But the dialectic says: *Those who still live must not say 'never'.* It says: *If lost, fight!* And it says: *The vanquished of today are the victors of tomorrow.* With these tried and tested slogans Brecht's poetry did not avoid the cruel prospects of fascism; it defied them.

The World-Historic Process

If we select from Brecht's writings the plays *The Mother* (based on Gorky) and *Saint Joan of the Stockyards* (set in Chicago) then we see the same world-historic antithesis as in the poems about the Moscow metro and the city of New York. In this volume of poems we find *Freedom and Democracy* written in 1947, describing the murderous anachronism of the West German fascist restoration. If we compare it with the *Reconstruction Song* or the *Peace Song* or the *Children's Hymn*, written in the same year, then we see the world-historic antithesis transferred to the battlefield of Germany. In the poem *Training the Millet*, already referred to, the world-historic process is shown in a Soviet example in which the antithesis of struggle is newly presented as being between man and nature. This fine poem is a peace poem, although it certainly does not ignore the invasion of the warlike hordes. It is pure nature poetry, although nature here is no quiet corner for inner feelings, but rather a challenge to man to be aware of his power. This poem also includes our fields, our changed land, our new peasants. And it has poetic greatness, since it makes the difficult simple, and makes joyful that which is serious — and because a statistical account of harvest returns is presented to us as an oddly mischievous and comforting triumphal song about mankind.

Collected Poems

In 1879 Theodor Storm wrote a letter to Gottfried Keller highly praising his "Abendlied", and demanding that a collection of poems must consist solely of such perfect works. Keller, a realist, replied that the praise pleased him, but that he believed that in order to get through life we needed some ballast too, and that he would have to try to save some ballast in his collection of poems. Brecht's *One Hundred Poems* also include not only the greatest. They show the stations of his development and change. They show how he got through life. It is the stamp of Brecht's poetry that the person of the poet is completely subordinated to the inexorable force of the message, but in the cause the personal note of the artistic coming-to-terms with life is quite unmistakable. The content-determined and realistically accented tone of these poems does not exclude the unlosable note of lasting worth.

The heights which Brecht the poet can scale can be seen in this book in two of the most beautiful German love poems: *Memories of Marie A.* and *The Lovers.* And we recognise this beauty just because we have long been introduced to it in the coarse-grained, substantive and simple language of his political poems of struggle, the poems on contemporary themes.

Brecht's rhythm does not make the language fluid, but rather dams and roughens it, so that it may withstand pressure and counter-pressure. But anyone who wants to experience how such a hardening makes it easier to solve the problems of the joyful play of language should read the perfect poem: *The Legend of the Creation of the Book Taoteking when Laotse was on his Way to Emigration.* The wisdom of Laotse, disposed in a friendly manner towards man and towards life, overcomes harshness; and in the same way the aesthetic wisdom of Brecht can say in a cheerful manner things worth knowing. Brecht's humour is the mode in which his determined social commitment can appear as the high art of friendliness towards man and life.

Bertolt Brecht the Director

1952

During rehearsals Bertolt Brecht sits in the auditorium. His work as a director is unobtrusive. When he intervenes it is almost unnoticeable and always in the "direction of flow." He never interrupts, not even with suggestions for improvement. You do not get the impression that he wants to get the actors to "present some of his ideas"; they are not his instruments.

Instead he searches, together with the actors, for the story which the play tells, and helps each actor to his strength. His work with the actors may be compared to the efforts of a child to direct straws with a twig from a puddle into the river itself, so that they may float.

Brecht is not one of those directors who knows everything better than the actors. He adopts towards the play an attitude of "know-nothingism"; he waits. You get the impression that Brecht does not know his own play, not a single sentence. And he does not want to know what is written, but rather how the written text is to be shown by the actor on the stage. If an actor asks: "Should I stand up at this point?", the reply is often typically Brecht: "I don't know." Brecht really does not know; he only discovers during the rehearsal.

Everything — position, movement, gesture — serves Brecht in telling the story of the play.

The story of Mother Courage and her children: Anna Fierling, sutler, known as Mother Courage, goes to the wars with her three children to make business. She loses her children one after another, and becomes poor. Unteachable, she travels on alone. This story is shown in the twelve scenes of the play, and each of the scenes is divided into a series of events. Brecht directs the play as though each of these small events could be extracted from the play and presented by itself. They are conscientiously presented, down to the smallest details.

Brecht once wrote: The word of the writer is only as sacred as it is true. The theatre is not the servant of the writer, but of society.

On Brecht's stage everything must be "true"; but he prefers a particular sort of truth, the truth which comes as a discovery. During the presentation he will point beamingly with outstretched hand at an actor who has just shown something special or something important in human nature or human circumstance.

Human circumstance is studied very exactly. At the beginning of the eighth scene of *Mother Courage*, for instance, a young peasant comes with his mother to the military camp to sell blankets. This is not just to demonstrate that the peasants are selling their blankets; it must be shown that they are doing it in the fourteenth year of the war, they are doing nothing unusual. But it is difficult for them to do what is usual, for the blankets are the final thing they have to sell, they are in fact indispensable. With what will they cover themselves in the night? How does the mother look at the sack containing the blankets which are so important for the family? How does the son take from his shoulder the sack with such important contents? And how does he swing it up again when he hears that peace has broken out, and understands that the blankets need not be sold?

The lessons taught by the theatre must also entertain. On Brecht's stage everything must be beautiful. The poor room of Pelagea Vlassova must be beautiful, and so must the arrangement of the workers in the factory yard, and the colours of the costumes of the middle-class women at the brass-purchasing centre.

You certainly do not note all this at the first glance.

Brecht stages his plays so that you still notice something new the tenth time. The more often you see the play, the richer it seems. Even when you know the play itself well, there is new pleasure in the arrangement, the gestures, the colours, et cetera.

Brecht demonstrates a lot, but only very short passages; he breaks off in the middle so as not to show anything completed. He does not prescribe anything, but encourages the fantasy and the imagination of the actor. He always imitates the actor to whom he is demonstrating, but without dissimulation. His attitude is: People of this sort often do this or that in such a way.

And all actors must, for a moment at least, have the eyes and the ears of the spectator. Brecht explains: In real life nobody goes about unobserved, so how can an actor go across the stage unobserved? "This is your moment," he calls to the actor, "don't let it get away. Now it's your turn, and to hell with the play." Naturally this must be a moment where the play demands or allows such treatment. And Brecht says: "All those taking part are interested in carrying forward the common cause, yours too. But then there is also your interest, which stands in a certain contradiction to this. Everything lives from this contradiction." He never allows an actor, that is to say a character in the play, to be sacrificed in the interests of the tension or the speed of the play.

Brecht is the most gratifying audience for his actors. The actor has the right to recognition for his good performance. A joke remains a joke, even on the twentieth time of telling, and the actor has the right to get a laugh. Otherwise he will assume that he produced the joke badly this time.

Brecht always finds something to give to the actor at the right time. There is no embarrassment because something is missing, no empty minute because something has to be considered. Even if the solution is not final, the actor is kept busy: the rehearsal runs without snags.

Brecht knows how to get along with actors. They do not

have to submit to his mood, but he gives a reason for the mood of each of them. If the actor has a "good day" then Brecht is insatiable: he gets all that is possible out of him, but almost unnoticeably and without exhausting the actor. If the actor is in a bad mood, Brecht leaves him alone; he never insists on something which cannot be easily produced.

Brecht works intensively but not strenuously. His good humour at rehearsals spreads to the actors. You notice his intention to be entertained.

His pleasure in fine gestures and genuine attitudes provokes the actors; they show more, in expectation of his appreciation.

Brecht hates long discussions during rehearsals, particularly psychological ones. During the more than two hundred hours of rehearsal for *The Tutor* there was not more than a total of perhaps fifteen minutes of discussion between the auditorium and the stage. In any case he always tries out all proposals. "Why explain the reasons? Show the proposals," and "Don't talk about it, do it," are what he says. If the proposal is good it is adopted. If a proposal is poor, the absence of applause convinces an actor better than a long argument would.

Brecht always speaks loudly, and shouts his suggestions to the actors, mainly from the auditorium, so that everyone can hear them. This does not interfere with the unobtrusive nature of his intervention. When directing he is surrounded by pupils. He immediately passes on their good suggestions, always naming the person responsible: "X says, Y suggests." In this way the work becomes the work of all.

He explains to his pupils: "If we are unable to get out of a play or a scene what is in it, we must guard against pushing in something that is not in it. Plays and scenes must not be overstrained. If something is of lesser importance it is still of importance. If you give it too much, then this lesser (but genuine) will be destroyed. In all plays there are weak scenes (and weaknesses in general). If the play as a whole is halfway good, then there is often a balance, difficult to detect but easy to disturb. Often, for instance, the dramatist wins particular strength for a scene from the weakness of the preceding scene. Sometimes the weakness of a scene serves to make visible something which differs from that which is shown. The speech delivered by Coriolanus' mother, with which she confronts her son who is marching on his own city, was probably intentionally made weak by Shakespeare; he did not want Coriolanus to be diverted from his plan by real reasons or by deep emotion, but rather through a certain indolence with which he indulged in an old habit. It would therefore be wrong to give Volumnia better arguments and thus to make the speech more convincing.

"On the other hand, our actors often have too little confidence in the play, in an interesting moment in the story, in a convincing sentence, etc.; and then they do not allow this factor, which is 'anyway' interesting, to have its proper effect. In addition a play needs to have passages which are less effective. No spectator can follow a complete performance with equal intensity; this must be taken into consideration."

Angelika Hurwicz
Brecht's Work with Actors
1955

This theme undoubtedly deserves more thorough treatment than present circumstances allow. Brecht is a great methodiser and teacher. But it may be useful for once to lay aside Brecht's theoretical work, the *Small Organon*, and to report simply on impressions received during practical work with Brecht. This in particular since the author herself six years ago approached with some trepidation the task of working with Brecht and his legendary methods of directing. It should be stated right at the start that the first impression of Brecht's work was that it was the normal work of direction, the only difference being perhaps that it was pursued with greater patience. It was only slowly that Brecht's characteristic quality as a director emerged from many details and gave a full picture.

This short study provides an opportunity to point out — and this is the most important thing to be said here — what an unfortunate misconception is contained in the contrast which is so commonly drawn between Brecht and Stanislavsky. Stanislavsky was a great man of the theatre, and so was Brecht. Both of them strove for truth on the stage. Instead of constructing an artificial contradiction between their ideas based on their writings on the subject, which unnecessarily confuses all young people attached to the theatre, it would be better to point out the ways in which they agreed. In the final analysis there can only be one truth. But before such a conciliatory investigation is undertaken it must be pointed out quite clearly that Stanislavsky, exclusively a director, naturally had a stronger interest in practising the smallest dramatic details than has Brecht, who is mainly a playwright and must therefore proceed with larger strides. It is not unimportant to emphasise that Stanislavsky began to develop his system in co-operation with Chekhov during the epoch of naturalism, and that Brecht established his system when he recognised that the theatre must depict the world as something which can be changed.

In a discussion on his work as director Brecht once stated that his aim was to show the mode of conduct of people in specific situations; it was irrelevant to him whether the actor was cold or hot in the process. This remark included the thought that Brecht is by no means hostile to drama exercises aimed at ensuring the truth to life and the warmth of the presentation of the role; in fact he regards them as a prerequisite. Brecht simply starts with what Stanislavsky calls the "super-task" of the actor.

Stanislavsky states at one point: "The aim, the target which I will attain, both as character in a play and as actor of a contemporary theatre, that is the basis of our art. This 'for what?' and 'which target' is always defined both by the ideals of the author and actor and in equal measure by the ideals of the epoch in which both author and actor live and create."

At another point he states: "But when will you [the actor] be able to proceed from the stage of skill and self-confidence as an actor to the stage of creation? At that point at which your human task appears, superior to all tasks on the stage; when you share the ideas of the author, when you experience them and include them in the action, warm them with your emotions and awaken new vital energies in the spectators. We shall give these tasks the name of the 'super-tasks' of the actor."

To return to Brecht: all that he said in the *Small Organon* against the possession of the actor by his role, which has caused so much confusion and indignation, is aimed against actors who forget about their super-task, who only see their own parts, and who offend against the content of the play as a whole, even when they give their parts interesting details and great acting ability.

Brecht's words that it is all the same whether an actor plays hot or cold, which may at first sight seem strange, and also the still unusual concept of "epic theatre", are the key to the recognition of the importance which Brecht has for a new generation of German actors. His work with young actors and weaker actors (theatre cannot be dependent upon great talents, for all plays have quite a number of parts) is of the very greatest educational importance.

To play epic theatre means to tell the story of the play. All the work is subordinated to this end. For Brecht the director it is therefore irrelevant which actor-individual plays a part. Brecht does not cast parts in accordance with individuality. He demonstrates persons as the product of the conditions in which they live, and capable of change through the circumstances which they experience. Abstract psychology is unimportant to Brecht. By an unusual and daring distribution of parts he expands the range and ability of many actors.

With actors who fail to produce a certain nuance necessary at a key-point in the plot, Brecht takes all possible measures to achieve his ends. He replaces emphasis by gesture, gesture by a pause, a look by a throat-clearing, and so on. In this way Brecht trains actors to be exact, to be responsible with regard to their parts and the whole play, without forcing them.

Brecht's method of inducing actors to abandon the often flexionless stage language is as simple as it is unusual. He encourages the actor to speak his lines in his native dialect. Feelings and thoughts often lose their originality of expression when they are pressed into the careful language of the stage. There is something analogous in the exercise of good manners, which prescribe that strong feelings should be manifested in measured language. Speaking in dialect, the actor expresses himself more freely; unexpected and unhackneyed tones emerge, which must then be transposed, purely musically, into Standard German.

It can be said that Brecht, in his treatment of speech on the stage, bases himself on the best naturalist traditions of the German stage, without allowing naturalisms.

It would be satisfying if these few remarks could make it clear that epic theatre is, in the main, the step from naturalism to realism. This is the explanation for its existence and its importance.

Paul Dessau
How Lucullus Came About
1963

I grew up with song. Singing has been a tradition in my family for a long time. My great-grandfather was a cantor, and he himself wrote many of the songs which he needed for the services. This my father told me, and his father too had been a cantor. My father was also destined by his father to become a cantor, since he had a particularly fine voice. However (as a result of events about which it would be interesting to write, but which would take us too far away from the subject), he became a cigar-maker; after work he sang in club choirs in smoke-filled rooms, but this could not affect his natural voice. As a boy I sang in a synagogue choir in Hamburg. I liked to play the violin and also to sing, so that my father, who was having me trained as a violinist, thought for a while that I should rather become a singer. Luckily I ruined my voice so thoroughly when it was breaking that I remained a violinist.

Whilst I was a student in Berlin a friend encouraged me to compose an opera. I was sixteen at the time. The story was veristic, a frightful love story; I collected all the music which I knew, that is to say all the way from Puccini to Richard Strauss, and stuffed all the parts which appeared suitable into this youthful construction. This was in 1910. It took me two years to create this "work"; I would not have mentioned it, had it not so much to do with my long-lasting and intimate relationship with opera.

It has always been difficult to find a good libretto for an opera. I made very many attempts. Grillparzer's "Der Traum ein Leben", Eichendorff's "Die Freier" (adapted by Otto Zoff), Upton Sinclair's novel "The Jungle"; I tried them all, carving out the text myself, but they all remained fragments.

In the 1920s I heard a lot about Brecht. *The Yes-Sayer*, a school opera by Brecht and Weill, which I heard in the Karl Marx School in Berlin, made an enormous impression on me. A short while later I heard *Lindbergh's Flight*, also by Brecht and Weill, in a concert version conducted by Otto Klemperer at the Kroll Opera. Then came *The Threepenny Opera*. But I knew very well that it was too early for me to speak to Brecht about working together on an opera subject. The text of my "Children's Cantata", which I wrote myself, proves on the one hand my own lack of independence, and on the other the influence which Brecht already exerted on me.

The first Brecht texts which I set to music were the songs in *99 %*, a series of scenes which later received the title *The Fear and Misery of the Third Reich*. The premiere with my music took place in Paris in 1938: Helene Weigel was one of the actors, Slatan Dudow directed. A little later I composed the *Song of the Black Straw Hats* for *Saint Joan of the Stockyards*; later this played the decisive role in the long period of joint work done by Brecht and me, beginning in New York in 1942.

At a Brecht Evening in a large New York hall, with Elisabeth Bergner and Peter Lorre amongst the cast, an Italian girl was due to sing the *Song of the Black Straw Hats*. Brecht had been pleased by my music. The singer cancelled her appearance on short notice. Brecht encouraged me to take her place, and to sing the song myself in the programme. He encouraged me with the words: "Eisler sometimes sings his songs himself too." It was on this evening that we arranged our first working discussion. Brecht suggested that I should write music for his poem *Oh Germany, Ashen Mother*. This then became the introduction to the choral "German Miserere". The work on "German Miserere" was finished shortly before we both returned to Germany. I remember that I received some of the texts from Brecht more or less as an afterthought, almost with embarrassment. For instance he gave me the poem *Song of a German Mother* while we were walking on Broadway, saying: "I composed one line myself." The few notes which he had "composed" he sang to me on the spot. Here they are:

hätt' ich ge-wußt, was ich heut weiß,

It is obvious that it is very difficult to include a phrase which has neither beginning nor end. I liked these two bars, and particularly the way that Brecht had produced them, so I made an effort, and thought and hummed to myself, in order to convert Brecht's two bars into eight, the number needed for the verse. I was soon able to play the song to Brecht, and I remember clearly that he liked it particularly.

Before he left New York, Brecht said: "Come to Hollywood too, we'll be able to work better there." It was easier said than done. Where should I get the fare? What would I live on in Hollywood? But there was a friendly solution, and it came fairly soon. A young director, with whom I had already worked in Paris, commissioned a small piece of film music from me. At this time I was earning my living as a worker on a chicken farm in New Jersey. I found time to compose as well as look after the chickens, and the work on the small film provided the fare to California.

I visited Brecht in his small white frame house in Santa Monica. We started to work as though there had been no interruption. "I've got a play here that you ought to read, because it must have music: *Mother Courage and Her Children.* Several songs need composing." And he began to read me the poems, quietly, gently, emphasising the meaning, and more musically than almost any poet can ever have read. And he gave me a small black photostated book, the text of *Mother Courage and Her Children.* Before this, Brecht had shown me a tune included in the *Music for Singing* in the appendix to his *Household Homilies.* This was the *Ballad of the Pirates*, a tune allegedly derived from the French: "L'Etandard de la Pitié", which Brecht had used as the model for the entrance song in *Mother Courage:* "Now captains, let the drums be rested." I was surprised at the banality of the tune, and at Brecht's suggestion, though it was made politely, that he would like it used for his song. "Big changes will be necessary to make this model usable for an important song," I said, and Brecht agreed. And this is the origin of the song "Now captains, let the drums be rested" in its present version. Mother Courage's song:

Ihr Haupt-leut, laßt   die Trom-mel ruh-en____

based upon the *Ballad of the Pirates*

This form of plagiarism was at that time quite strange to me. Today I regard it not only as legitimate, but also as natural and fruitful. While I was composing for *Mother Courage* and doing other work — Helene Weigel had suggested the "Kriegslied" by Matthias Claudius, and there was the first portion of the "German Miserere" — Brecht read to me passages from *The Interrogation of Lucullus*, a radio play he had written in Denmark in 1939. I can still recall clearly the pleasure with which he read the verses from the *Farewell of the Living*, which later became a quintet in my opera. It is a poem in which the rhymes may be said to run between your legs, trapping you if you look at them closely. The first rhyme (for "Lakalles") — Brecht roared with laughter at this nickname for the Roman general — occurs in the fifth line; the second rhyme (for "Bock") comes in the seventh line, and so on. It was soon plain to me what Brecht was aiming at: he wanted to have the radio play "be-operaed". In the following days I paid a lot of attention to the text. There were many passages which lent themselves well to dramatic composition, but for a long time I could not see how we could make an opera out of it. Then the theme faded from our conversations for a lengthy period.

One day Brecht asked me whether I knew Stravinsky. I told him that a performance of his "'Histoire du Soldat'' was due soon in the Hollywood area, and that I would probably speak to Stravinsky there. Brecht then asked me to draw Stravinsky's attention to *Lucullus*, which he believed would be a good opera text. Apparently Brecht had stricken me from his list with regard to this plan. I gave Brecht's message to Stravinsky. He refused, saying that he was over-burdened with work for the next two years. Until 1948, the year which brought Brecht and myself together again in Zurich, nothing more was said about *Lucullus*.

We were in Berlin. The preparations for the first night of *Mother Courage* were in full swing. At lunch time one day I was sitting in the club "Möwe" at one table, and Brecht was sitting with Director S. at another. Brecht called across to me: "Dessau, you can get a commission for an opera. S. wants to have *The Interrogation of Lucullus* for the North-west German Radio as a radio opera. There'll be a big advance." A radio opera! An advance! I had no money and no commissions, and agreed. "The contract will be ready shortly."

The contract never was ready. But I have to thank this vague offer for stimulating me to considering that the apparatus for a *Lucullus* opera should not be too large, that it should be based on a small orchestra. These ideas led me straight to working on the music for a proper opera.

And then the difficulties began to pile up, difficulties which had already made me think twice in Santa Monica. Right up to the final rehearsal Brecht worked untiringly to help master these difficulties. During the course of work we realised that the radio-play version would have to be changed in many ways. Much had to be looked at anew and written anew, much had to be removed and new material provided. With Brecht, intervention and changes always meant enrichment. This is shown even in the change in the title. Instead of the radio-play title of *The Interrogation of Lucullus* it is now called "The Condemnation of Lucullus". Or we may take the first scene, to which three female heralds were added, who, with their phrases of devotion, provided the contrast so necessary for this scene (as the sonata form shows). The new and unique feature of this collaboration was that the important changes, which were necessary so that the radio play could develop into an opera libretto, always produced new qualities.

When I asked Brecht to change the conclusion, he did not happen to be in Berlin. As usual, he did not answer my letter. But he gave his answer immediately after his return, with a concluding scene which ends with these classical lines which apply to the war criminals of all times and all countries:

> *Yes, into the void with him! How long*
> *Shall they, he and his like,*
> *Throne inhuman over people, raising*
> *Their idle hands, and hurling*
> *Peoples one against another in bloody wars?*
> *How long more*
> *Shall we and ours endure them?*
> *Yes, into the void with him, and into the void*
> *With all his like.*

Manfred Wekwerth
Discovering
an Aesthetic Category
1957

Our last discussions with Brecht concerned the production
of his play *The Days of the Commune*. Rehearsals were due
to start in mid-September in Karl-Marx-Stadt, and there
were still many problems. This was during the beautiful
August days last year, and we found him in his gardener's
house in Buckow in the best of spirits, which made work
difficult. This forced us repeatedly to block Brecht's daring
attempts to break out, to jump from the hundredth to the
thousandth.

We had talked for a good half hour about co-determina-
tion for the workers in their factories before we were able
to awaken Brecht's curiosity for the story of his play:

In besieged Paris in 1871 big business and small business
no longer flourishes. The bourgeoisie are corrupt to the very
marrow...

Then Brecht interrupted: there was the story of Widow
Cabet and her son, as far as he could recall, they had something to do with cockades. What happened to them?

It was not easy to satisfy the demands of our listener:
they were at too low a level. He wanted to be entertained,
at all costs. If his demands were met he was the sort of
listener that Brecht the playwright and Brecht the director
always praised: ready to be taught, if the teaching was
mixed with amusement.

But it was a new sort of amusement which we were expected to provide. It is difficult to describe at the typewriter,
but it can be seen in any inn. There taxi driver So-and-So
submits to his audience for their approval the naked details
of his latest conflict with the traffic police. It was ridiculous

to claim his lights weren't good enough! Much is demanded of the listener: every detail, every piece of the event must be assessed. A global answer would be rejected as unqualified. The event is the main thing, not opinions about it. Engineers, judges, historians are challenged, continually and sharply. And woe betide if, after a favourable reply, the expected "Absolutely right" is not pronounced, or if the sentence "When they're in the right, they're in the right" is omitted after the just objection of the opponent has been mentioned. Much is demanded of the narrator: from all the things which happened he has to select just that artistic selection which will put his listeners in the state of productive consumption. This is the soul of the whole affair.

Pursuing the story of Madame Cabet, we recounted roughly as follows: In besieged Paris in 1871 big business and small business no longer flourishes. In a small café which now serves as recruiting station for the National Guard, a plump gentleman complains to the waiter about the present barrenness of the war, and Madame Cabet, the seamstress with an unemployed son on her hands, cannot dispose of her cockades. By chance she detects, in a group of the National Guardsmen returning from a sortie, her lodger. With fiscal implacability she who is kicked passes on the kick: in the name of the government she demands the immediate payment of back rent. But François cannot meet the bill; his pay is just enough for a glass of wine, and in addition he has been wounded. His comrades manage to bribe Madame Cabet with a chicken left behind by the gentleman who fled at the sight of the Guardsmen. Madame Cabet mentions that just by chance she has not had a proper meal, and her son Jean detracts from the ceremonious feast with the news that those inside no longer took the cockades because the government did not want to see even more workers under arms. Madame Cabet has to lay the half-eaten chicken in her basket, because the Guards recognise in her an ally against the treacherous government. They march off to demonstrate outside the town hall. After this demonstration governmental circles are sensitive to the sound of marching feet. With no delay they wish to conclude peace with the Prussians. This open national treachery mobilises the proletariat, who turn their weapons the other way. The national struggle is converted into social struggle. Revolution . . .

"Stop, not so quickly," says Brecht, getting his oar in. "I don't understand. Who does the converting? The proletariat are armed in the National Guard, and follow the national slogans of the bourgeoisie. When the bourgeoisie sabotage the defence, the proletarians demonstrate, and rub these slogans, national slogans, under the noses of the bourgeoisie. How does the change-over to social struggle take place? You must have omitted something."

We knew the play by heart, and it was not easy for us to tell the story naked and "one thing after another." The events can easily suffer at the hand of the noteworthy, that which is worthy-of-note. A contradiction evaporates very soon. We had long manoeuvred (which is also necessary) to provide the answers before the questions were posed. Brecht regarded such an approach as tactless. It not only bored him: it put him in a bad humour. He did not like things to be pre-chewed; this robbed him of the joy of eating. He interpreted the sentence "Truth is concrete" in a productive way: by long practice he had made himself incapable of understanding dry abstractions. He spoke with malice of the way in which people attempted to find the common denominator for the lively variety, the innumerable shades, the moving unrest of contradictions and disharmonies. For him everything was "theatre": the unbending men of character, merciless fate, the ideas which consumed all life — a monster similar to Luther's Anti-Christ. He spat on them and on those who popularised them. Such a lowly activity as telling a story could make extraordinarily concrete the wisdom of the sentence "to ascend to the concrete."

The conversion took place in the third scene, we replied to Brecht, the scene in which the popular rising breaks out.

In the fourth scene the revolution — unexpectedly for the revolutionaries — has suddenly arrived. Brecht: "What actually happens in the third scene?"

This was a genuine question. Brecht had developed the art of forgetting; he acted so much as a stranger towards his friends that they were continually being surprised.

In this scene a queue of women are standing at five in the morning in front of a bakery. They mistrust the sudden ration of white bread announced by the government. With the bread already in their arms they discover the regular soldiers stealing their cannon. There is nearly a duel between François of the National Guard and his brother Philippe, a regular soldier. Madame Cabet's intervention prevents it, and the women seduce the soldiers into fraternisation. The cannon is saved. Together the National Guard, the women and the regular soldiers march on the town hall: the revolution has arrived. The fourth scene shows the Central Committee at its constituent session.

Our audience appeared to have achieved what he wanted: he had ceased to listen. He was still astonished at the action taken by Monsieur Thiers: it was a crazy idea for a government to try to steal the cannon of a whole *arrondissement* quietly at night. One could, for instance, show the advancing soldiers less as soldiers and rather as gangsters. The gang leader could peer round the corner first and beckon on his followers with exaggerated silent-film gestures. The heavily armed detachment could then appear on tiptoe, comical and threatening at one time. Recovering his breath after his laughter, Brecht suggested that the women who caught the cannon-thieves might also have something of this laughter. After all, they were proletarians and they would know how to judge the cunning of Monsieur Thiers, famous from the schoolbooks. Then again the danger of the situation would have to be shown.

Brecht stretched idly in his cane chair: he always found it astonishing how quickly soldiers forgot their oath of loyalty when there were women around, even the toughest soldiers. This fact was not well enough known.

Mainly in order to hold off the threatening breakout, we interrupted with a question (Azdak: ". . . and there is nothing more tempting than a question."): Which is more productive for this scene — if the women in the queue regard the government's white bread merely as political white bread, or if they also see it as a means of staving off their hunger? Brecht begins to listen bad-temperedly. We continue the attack: Is it a good thing for the women to be mistrustful "in principle" of any bread from the government? In this case the scene would simply confirm a well-known mistrust: in fact Thiers provided the white bread only in order to steal the cannon. Would it not be more fruitful here (we continued our provocation) to apply the dialectical "not — but"? Brecht's reply: could we lend him a copy of the text? He took off his glasses and studied the text with puckered face. He took his ballpoint, scribbled a few lines, made a few rapid deletions. Then he handed back the text, suggesting this might be better.

As a result of his tiny change the scene took a completely new course. At the start the women in the queue still speak mistrustfully about the government's white bread. But Geneviève the teacher, a "political" person, argues so sharply that she provokes the others into saying: "If Thiers' peace tastes of bread, then I am for it," and "Bread is bread." It is only when the government takes action, in the form of stealing the cannon, that the various opinions form one front: against the government. When they go into action against the soldiers the women have the white bread in their arms. "Once again we see," said Brecht as he put away his ballpoint, "the dialectical solution is always more lively, more diverse, more naive."

Brecht likes to pronounce maxims like this. Wiseacres therefore try to reconstruct a model of Brecht's mode of thinking or his thought-production by assembling such maxims. They point to his example when accused of the lavish use of maxims. In fact intimidation by means of a hail of maxims is spreading here like the Great Plague once spread in London. Whole plays are packed with them; critics hack them out like lumberjacks fell trees; the newspapers sometimes consist almost entirely of judgments and condemnations. It is, however, much harder to describe something than to judge it. Brecht used his maxims for a very practical purpose: he packed into them a lot of concrete material which would then be handy at all times. When he pronounced a maxim then a whole heap of experiences, events, jokes, stories and contradictions fell apart like the sticks in the Japanese game of Mikado. His facility in this direction allowed him to make great leaps from one subject to another. He found pleasure in the fickleness of thought. His maxims did not produce a standstill but speedier movement: they were not full stops but colons. Incidentally it annoyed him if he was countered by one of his "absolutes" of yesterday: he denied it because it had become unreal. Brecht had no peer in promoting to a constructive mode of work the despised phrase: "He marched them up to the top of the hill, and he marched them down again."

We transferred to our texts the changes in the third scene. Brecht used the opportunity to follow up with some pleasure a thought: "There is no purely theoretical access to our mode of playing theatre. It would be a good idea to publish unusually lively examples of the dialectical mode of playing, I mean our unusually fine photographs of *Chalk Circle*. Would you note this?" He developed a plan to publish about twenty of the best photographs with descriptions. The descriptions should be in the style of his descriptions of the pictures of Brueghel, displaying the contradictions in poetic form. Apart from its aesthetic charm this would have an educational effect for actors.

Since we had arrived at *Chalk Circle* we wanted to grasp the opportunity. We were worried about the tempo of *Chalk Circle* and *Courage* for the London tour. Despite big cuts the stop watch results were alarming.

And then there was the Underground, the anxiety of the British about temporary aberrations in the German arts, the language problem. We asked for a few lines for the actors. Brecht sat down at the typewriter and quickly typed a short letter, querying us about an occasional formulation: On the London Tour. He rolled it out of the machine and read it to us for confirmation. I wish I could describe the "tone" of this sentence: "Secondly, there exists in Britain an old fear that German art (literature, painting, music) is frightfully ponderous, slow, fussy and pedestrian."

Today I cannot recall the whole course of our conversation so well that I could name in the right order the various points which were dealt with between the hundredth and the thousandth. For the *Commune* I noted at one point: *The Commune* must be played naively.

It was getting near to midday when Brecht extracted, from under a wobbling pile of papers and books, three stapled pages: on his advice his son had written down fifty popular sentences of dialectic, and we should check whether they would be useful in the theatre. Brecht had been speaking much in this period about dialectics in the theatre. He generally called his theatre now "dialectical theatre". We closed our *Commune* books.

In fact dialectic for the theatre must be regarded anew, more practically. For him dialectic was the chance to show an event in a living way. Brecht noticed that I was taking a note: "Underline the word *living* very thickly! There are idiots who always confuse dead and living." And in the conventional theatre this idiocy is particularly deeply rooted, Brecht continued in his provocative manner; in the conventional theatre special craftsmanship is applied in order to clear the ground of the "unevennesses", that is to say the contradictions, of the plot. But a clear ground is an empty ground. For this reason it was impossible to attach too much importance to the demand that events should be depicted in a lively way, however easy this might sound. For his theatre work the whole of philosophy was only interesting to him to the extent that it helped in the lively presentation of social processes. However, he prized liveliness just as highly as Lenin did in his last writings on dialectic.

Brecht walked to and fro as he talked. His fury disappeared as quickly as it had come. When he sat down again he asked us how we liked the term "dialecticise". For practical work, he added. In your work you must always investigate an event in order to discover its process. For instance: why is this and that lively? In this manner you can keep the event in movement, keep it alive, for by the process of "dialecticising" you have discovered the moving contradictions of an event. This is also true in judging a work of art. Telling the story on the stage is, in the final analysis, a "dialecticisation" of the events. In everyday life the force of habit mostly kills the liveliness of the events observed. Correct observation is also "dialecticisation", a re-awakening. And Brecht closed his short, wild, enjoyable improvisation about the dialectic with the malicious words: "Dialecticisation is, in the final analysis, a matter of feeling."

We already had our brief cases in our hands when one of Brecht's discoveries held us back. He had always been surprised that it was so difficult to talk to people about his theatre theories. Even friends spoke of something quite other than what he meant. Where he said "X" people understood "U". At the start he had blamed his formulations, but the simpler he made the formulations, the greater the misunderstandings. The real reason must be: in formulating his theories he had omitted one half, assuming that this was obvious in the theatre — the role of the naive.

Brecht said this quite naively, without irony. It was, for him, a real discovery. He was seriously surprised that for years his theatre had been regarded un-naively. He was startled: "Most people who deal with the theatre — and not only the theoreticians — do not even have this word in their vocabulary. How can they make worth-while, living theatre?" Brecht had always been relentlessly opposed to

the newer experiments in Marxist aesthetics, but now he had
caught them in a state of ignorance about the naive. "They
really believe that there can be great beauty in art without
naivety. The naive is an aesthetic category, the most concrete category."

We knew the word "naive" from Brecht's rehearsals, in
which he often shouted it to the actors on the stage. But this
was the first time we had heard it from him in such a general
context. We asked him how he imagined a definition of the
naive. The thought of having to give a definition at the drop
of a hat was apparently upsetting; we could do this if we
wished. He could only cite examples of successful naive
performances as they occurred to him. I noted the scanty
examples:

Naive: The representation of the whole population of
Rouen in *Jeanne d'Arc* by a small group of seven persons.

Naive: the altered course of scene three in the *Commune*.

Naive: the appearance of a figure just when you can say:
here comes so-and-so. Or when you can say: now this-and-
that is going to happen.

The depiction of historical events by Brueghel is naive,
for instance "The Fall of Icarus".

The opposite of naive presentation is naturalism.

Brecht could not make up his mind to answer a question
as to whether Molière's presentation of comic situations was
naive or not. To our astonishment he claimed that there
were naive elements in Hegel's analytical presentations, but
denied there were in his speculative presentations. As a
classical example of naive presentation in political literature,
Brecht cited Lenin's suggestions for climbing mountains.
"The presentation of the *Commune* must have something of
this naivety."

The advantage of such discoveries of Brecht's, for instance
of naivety, was that they were off-beat. Their use could
never be grasped immediately, because they appeared to be
charging open doors; naivety is something self-evident. It
was only afterwards, when we were staging the *Commune*,

that this open door slammed shut in our faces; we had to open it all over again. Only then did we note that we were passing through a door. Naivety became a problem.

Brecht was an ideal teacher, that is to say an uncomfortable teacher. He nagged away so long at self-evident facts, ready solutions, perfections and other agreeable things that you began to get fed up with them. So you rejected them and looked at them uneasily with a fresh eye; and the self-evident facts, the solutions, the perfections, suddenly became problems.

"Naivety is the whole undertaking of our mode of playing," said Brecht, returning to the problems of our theatre. "In our performances we tell the plot, the direct story. There can be or there should be artistic acts, ideas, but the main thing is the telling of a notable event." We objected that in our plays we were presenting a differentiated, detailed theatre. Brecht considered this to be not an exclusive contradiction, but a productive one: "Undifferentiated naivety is primitive." In addition, he added, we were not presenting a differentiated soul-massage, but differentiated observations of the conduct of man. The term psychology should be interchangeable with knowledge of human nature, at least in the theatre.

A gong sounded, the conversation was interrupted in mid-sentence; it was lunch time. At the table Brecht talked about all sorts of things; he had long forgotten the discussion. Because we had so many questions we utilised the first opportunity to continue the conversation with Brecht, one hour after lunch. To our astonishment he would not listen to us, but started talking about the *Commune*. Earlier, he said, we had not told the story of the first scenes naively, we had told it ironically. We tried to ask him whether irony and naivety were mutually exclusive. He overlooked our question, and went on to say that political plays, in particular, demanded a naive presentation. The story must be told directly, not indirectly:

Madame Cabet, the seamstress, takes cockades every day

to the recruiting office of the National Guard / her son Jean, an engine driver, rejects a commission from a plump gentleman / a group of National Guardsmen, returning from a sortie and on their way to demonstrate outside the town hall, discover that their pay scarcely suffices for a glass of wine / the plump gentleman is enraged about the Guardsmen who think about their pay in the midst of the patriotic struggle. He flees / Madame Cabet has not sold her cockades; she is faced with ruin / Madame Cabet sees amongst the Guardsmen her lodger François, who has been wounded, and demands from him his long-owed rent, etc.

The jump from the hundredth to the thousandth had been worth-while. From this viewpoint the hundredth could be seen in a new fashion.

Stage Technicians Relate

1957

Gerhart S., chief technician

I had the opportunity to talk to Brecht when he wanted to know about technical points. With other directors you don't get such close contact, but Brecht had every phase shown to him directly by the worker. He paid heed to things that other directors leave to the stage designer or the technical director.

— Did you ever have a row with Brecht? —

Years ago. We were rehearsing "Katzgraben"; *Courage* was to be shown in the evening. At 5 p.m. I drew Brecht's attention to the fact that we had to re-fit the stage for the evening performance, and he said: "Just ten minutes more, S." When I drew his attention to the time half an hour later he got impatient and said: "I'll rehearse till everything is right." He was not thinking about the evening performance, but only about the rehearsal. When I asked him once again to stop there was a row. Brecht cancelled the performance, and rehearsed through the evening. But that was an exception, with "Katzgraben" shortly before the first night. Generally Brecht settled everything in good humour.

I remember a rehearsal which was being run by the assistants. We had constantly to re-arrange the sets, and we did not like it. When new instructions came, I shouted into the auditorium: "You really ought to make up your minds." From the laughter I noticed that the latest instructions were from Brecht, who had arrived in the meantime. But Brecht himself laughed very much.

I was particularly struck by the fact that for Brecht the technical equipment, like the revolving stage and the flies, were like living things. In other theatres you build three or four sets on the revolving stage, and then turn one to the front. Brecht used it as a dramatic element — for Grushe's climb through the mountains, for Mother Courage's journey to the wars — marking a change in place or time. Probably it was this which made technical things so important for him.

We were amused by the fact that Brecht did not allow anything to stop his cigar, not even the firemen. When a picture appeared in a magazine showing Brecht in the audience with a cigar, we showed it to the firemen. He couldn't be parted from his cigar.

Gerhard R., electrician

Brecht was a very simple person. If you met him in the yard, he might be deep in conversation but he was never so wrapped up that he overlooked one of the workers. He said good morning to a cleaning woman from twenty yards away: the workers soon noted this. Once he was standing in the yard with his old "Steyr" car — he still drove the old heap — and a bricklayer who was working on something said to him: "Tell your old man he ought to get a new bus." Brecht simply laughed and said: "It still runs quite well."

When I didn't have anything to do backstage I used to sit down near Brecht and try to listen to what they were saying at the director's desk. When there was a misunderstanding on a technical point, I sometimes let drop a word. Then Brecht turned round right away and asked: "What's your opinion? Say just what you think." He was ready to listen to any objection . . .

Werner L., chauffeur and later stage craftsman

— When you were driving Helene Weigel, and sometimes Brecht, he often sent you to rehearsals, is that right? —

Yes, he always discussed lots of things. He often took advice, which I wouldn't have expected. He always asked me what I didn't agree with, not only in the theatre but with our government and our laws. Then he used to explain how the time had not yet come for a lot of things, and said that the time would come. We often used to talk about his plays.

— I remember you sitting in on the rehearsals of
    The Mother, that was in 1950. —

Yes, I was supposed to go to the rehearsals and make sure that everything was right. First I said it wasn't right that the comrade gave Pavel the jacket when he had to flee. Frau Weigel playing Vlassova should do it, that's what a mother does. Brecht said right away: "Yes, that's good," and changed it. In the "Broken Jug" something was changed too. They wanted to put up two clothes posts in the kitchen. "People don't do that," I said, "the washing should be put by the stove." So they hung the washing on a line by the stove."

Helmut M., property-master

— You worked with Brecht before 1933 on the production of *The Mother*? —

Yes, on *The Mother* in 1932, and some political revues. I was with an amateur group, and Brecht's troupe needed me for advice. The titles between the scenes appeared on a screen at the side mechanically, and something was sticking. I said: "You'll have to do it by hand, the hand is the most reliable machine, and anyway it's cheaper." We hadn't got any money in those days, we were playing theatre under the most difficult conditions. A brass curtain rail and a couple of laths, that was the whole business. In the butcher's scene, for instance, we used a margarine keg as a chopping block, with a couple of legs underneath. The audience noticed it, of course, but Brecht said it didn't matter.

Even then Brecht used to do odd things, particularly technically.

When the titles had to be turned on, we had to give a signal, and this was difficult. The set-painter had to sit in the front row of the audience with a string in his hand, and when he pulled a bell sounded backstage. I wanted to take a dark-coloured string so you couldn't see it, but Brecht demanded a light one so it could be seen. So we bought a washing-line.

Frau Weigel, who played the Mother, clapped her hands each time when things had to start up again, like in a lantern lecture.

If anything was missing, a chair or something, Brecht himself went to the cellar to choose one. We had no stage workers, simply an old man who looked after the hall, a sort of custodian. Brecht himself carried up a cupboard or whatever it was.

I'm not really a stage expert. When Brecht got me in 1932, I was unemployed; I was really a confectionery worker. Through Brecht and the amateur group I took up theatre full-time. Brecht took a lot of trouble to see to it that I got a job; it was frightfully difficult in those days. He wrote a number of letters on my behalf.

Brecht was always interested in what we thought about his work. In *The Mother* there was a verse about the police and the soldiers "who get 'a lot' of money and are ready to do anything." I said I didn't agree they got a lot of money, a worker earned more than a policeman; and I happened to know that the man who murdered Rosa Luxemburg was signing on at the labour exchange in the Gormann Strasse. He couldn't have got much for the murder. Anyway some workers had waited for him in the evening and beaten him up. So Brecht changed the text and it then went "who get 'little' money but are ready to do anything." Brecht was an individualist, I would say, but he always questioned many people and checked his ideas.

— How long have you been with Brecht again? —

Since January 1954, since we have our own theatre. I visited Frau Weigel in the Deutsches Theater, and after that we kept in touch. She always said: "When we have a theatre of our own, then you'll rejoin us." I still had some material from before 1933, things for the sets. I had kept it, after all it was people's property. And in the props box I still had things from before 1933; now they belong to our theatre.

(Incidentally M. placed in Brecht's grave a piece of the red flag from the 1932 production of *The Mother* which he had kept through the Nazi period.)

— Did Brecht recognise you? —

Of course. He said right away: "You used to be the stage manager." (I wasn't just the props man, I did that too, and scene-shifting, everything technical.) Brecht hadn't changed at all — he was just as he had been twenty-five years earlier.

Eduard F., prop-maker and theatrical sculptor

When I started here, Frau Weigel was looking for somebody who could make a hen for *Courage*. I was almost insulted when she demanded that I should make a hen; anybody could do that, I thought. But she wanted a particular sort of hen, one that she could pluck. It should be possible to pluck the feathers and then replace them. That was a frightful job, I said, and it would cost a lot of money. When I then demonstrated the hen to her, she fell on my neck; but I was really not satisfied. I was annoyed afterwards that I hadn't made the hen better.

— At what stage of the production did Brecht talk to you about your work? —

Before the production. I thought it was fine: he let us have our say. Brecht never laid down: "I want it just like this." Everybody who worked on the job could offer his opinion. Brecht looked at most of my products in my workshop. I still had three days' work to do on the big angel for "Urfaust", but Brecht said it was fine, get it out. For the witch on the roof I had to make seven drafts. I saw her as a fury, an old woman riding on a broomstick, with slippers, billowing skirts, flying hair — and Brecht had pictured her in just the same way.

— Did you have any differences? —

Well, when I made the Commander for *Don Juan*. I had a different idea of a fifty-year-old Frenchman than Brecht had, and I made mine. The Commander which I thought right was the one that came on the stage. When my name was called I prepared myself for the coming row, but Brecht congratulated me on my Commander.

— Didn't Brecht want the Commander to be deformed in some way, and not "handsome"? In Rostock he had liked the fact that his back was quite flat, like a bug, and didn't you afterwards make the back flat here too? —

That happened by accident. During the transport to Rostock the Commander got squashed flat, and it was just this that pleased Brecht. (F.'s Commander is over three metres tall, walks, speaks and nods.)

In Brecht's study I once put up the curtains on metal rings running on thin wires. Brecht was horrified when I mounted a handsome oaken lath in front. "You are covering up the whole technical apparatus. You have to see how it works." So we took the lath away.

When I once restored his Konfutse, the Chinese scroll in his apartment, he presented me with his plays with the dedication: *For saving Konfutse.*

Anton S., model-carpenter

— Did you ever have a row with Brecht? —

Row? Me? We got on marvellously, I never had a better boss all my life. When Brecht came to the rehearsal stage he always came to my workshop and had me show him what I was working on. He was interested in every smallest thing. He was here a few days before he died and asked about my work. Brecht always said that we were not just working for the few years in which our plays would be on the programme; in thirty or fifty years to come people would take out our stage models and study how we built our sets.

When I started here, nobody knew that I could build models. When Brecht found out, he didn't allow me to do a single stroke more in the big workshop; I immediately got my own small workshop, and my contract was altered. In the meantime my models have been shown at a lot of exhibitions in Paris, London, Vienna, and also in America.

Once I had made a model, Brecht wanted to have everything on the stage just like my model: the way the wood was handled, the shade of colour. I then had to work on the original sets, with shoe polish for example, or sandpaper, until everything was just right. During the preparatory discussions I had to be there right from the start.

In the five years we worked together, I never heard an unfriendly word from Brecht. He was more friendly to me than anybody before in any firm.

It's a bad thing that Brecht is no longer here — for me too. Who is there now who has such understanding for my work?

(Recorded by Käthe Rülicke-Weiler)

Erwin Strittmatter
Journeyman Years
with Brecht
1958

Although I was often with Brecht in the last years of his
life, worked with him, and had many long talks with him,
I find it difficult to write about him. He is too near to me,
and will always remain near. When working, dealing with
people, taking artistic decisions I often catch myself, and am
glad to catch myself, thinking: How would he have solved
that? How would he have acted here?

So I can see now how he would slap his knee (rather
carefully because of the fine ash on the cigar in his right
hand) when I say to him:

"Brecht, I don't feel well."

"I'll call a doctor right away."

"Not like that: I've got to write ten pages about the
human side of Brecht. The specialists are writing their ten
pages about the other sides of Brecht." And I can hear him
shouting between crows of laughter: "Write: He loved an
old car, meetings that did not last longer than one hour,
theatre in the morning and cheese in the evening."

Now that Brecht is dead I sometimes hear people speaking about "his greatness", people who earlier only talked
about his "curious cap" and his "impossible haircut". "It's all
very well and good, his *Mother Courage*, but how can he go
to a first night in a suit like that?"

I got to know Brecht like this: After my first novel I wrote
a play about peasants and gave it to the Potsdam Committee
for the World Youth Festival in Berlin. It was turned down
by an unknown jury. I asked for a discussion, from which I
might have learned something, but got no reply. I was very
depressed, for I was a beginner, a learner, not a master like

Brecht, who certainly knew how to stand up for the cause of art. The anonymous criticism was an icy douche for my creative energy.

Helene Weigel and Brecht, who had read my novel "Ochsenkutscher", learned about my play. I got a telegram from Helene Weigel asking me to submit the play to her. I had seen several Brecht productions and had a lot of respect for Brecht's art. That the Berliner Ensemble would occupy themselves with an attempt at a play by me I regarded as an enchanting mistake. I wanted to save both the dramaturgy department and Helene Weigel from this. I lied a little: the play was not yet finished, I was re-writing it. I really was re-writing it.

After a short while I got a second telegram. "What's up with the play?" Once again I could not make up my mind to submit it. "Re-writing again," I telegraphed back, and I really was doing this, because the play pleased me less and less. There followed a telegram from Brecht, and one day later a phone call: "Please don't re-write the play. First let us look at it together."

I could no longer get out of it. I took my play to Berlin, and handed it in. Brecht was not there, he had gone to the doctor. Aha, I said to myself, I know all about that. He wants to see what the play is like. Next week there will be a letter starting "We regret." I should take a look at a rehearsal and wait for Brecht, they said. The rehearsal is just intended as a cooling poultice, I thought after a quarter of an hour. I'll make it easy for him, instead of sitting around here and lurking. I left.

Three days later came a telegram: "Play accepted. Please come for discussion." So I ran into the wood, because you can't shout in the streets of a small town without being taken for a lunatic. "This can't be possible," I shouted, "the critics in Potsdam didn't like it, but Brecht does."

A few days later I was sitting facing him in the Luisen Strasse. I now saw the man about whom I had heard so many untruths (as I discovered in the first few weeks). The conversation went to and fro. I got to know his hard working clever assistants. I soon realised that my play might have been accepted, but that a lot of work still had to be done on it. Above all, Brecht wanted to see the first version. He knew very well why. Work — naturally, I wanted to. Now I could have a master who could tell me something binding. I may have gone pale from inner pleasure. During my talk with the staff of the dramaturgy department I could feel several times how Brecht observed me quite sharply, with a look as quick as a camera shutter. This glance combined appraisal and challenge. Later I was often able to observe it. But I may well have observed Brecht in the same manner while he was speaking to others. We were both watching (in a good sense) the other.

He apologised. He had really been absent when I delivered the manuscript, and had arrived just after I left. When our conversation had to be interrupted because of an urgent foreign call, he took me into an adjoining room, gave me some newspapers, and made sure that I was sitting comfortably. I found all this unusual, and it really was unusual. It is impossible to praise Brecht's politeness too much. The night before a lengthy journey which I later made with him he phoned suggesting I should take slippers and a comfortable pullover for the long car ride. He often interested himself in the smallest affairs of friends and acquaintances and gave advice, and not just casually. In this case I found his advice a little too avuncular, and took neither slippers nor a comfortable pullover. Out of politeness he therefore left his "comforts" in his case. I still regret this.

But to return to our first meeting. Perhaps what I am now about to write seems a little mystical; but other friends have confirmed my impression. When I said good-bye to him for the first time he looked at me unusually sharply and piercingly. At one stroke I felt the strength of his personality and knew that now I had to prove myself.

What followed was the richest period of development of all my previous life. We worked partly in Brecht's cottage in Buckow, and partly in Berlin. Not a minute of this time was without profit for me.

When the rehearsals began, I lived for more than three months at Brecht's house in Berlin-Weissensee. We stayed up together in the evening, and in the morning (sometimes literally in our underpants) told each other the ideas and thoughts which had come to us in the night. After we had worked in the morning for an hour or two we drove together to the theatre, talking philosophically on the way, or passing to each other our ideas about certain situations in the play "Katzgraben". Sometimes I got very frightened in the car when he took his hands from the wheel, but Brecht drove unusually safely, and despite our temperamental conversation I never saw him offend against the traffic regulations.

Once we needed an additional song between one rehearsal and the next. It had become usual that I wrote in the night changes in the text, or new passages. In the morning we went through the work together. This time I had found, during the night, nothing except the theme for a song. In the morning Brecht asked me for the new song. I was as embarrassed as a schoolboy who hasn't done his homework. "I haven't got anything yet, Brecht," I confessed, "but it might go like this . . ." I recited the first line. He immediately supplied the second, I the third, he the fourth, and so on. And so that morning one of the "Katzgraben" songs was created. It was a happy quarter of an hour in which we walked to and fro in the room, tossing lines at one another.

My collaboration with Brecht, my journeyman period with him, remains to be written about. It was sometimes a hard time, but more often gay. I learned more than I had in my previous forty years.

I shall attempt to indicate how he dealt with people, an art which is in a bad way here.

If somebody said to him: "So-and-so has said something nasty about you. So-and-so is going round spreading such-and-such a frightful lie about you," then he listened with a characteristic twitching of his neck muscles. He seldom made any comment, but he generally immediately invited such scandal-mongers to visit him. Thus it came about that people who least expected it received an invitation from Brecht. He was then particularly charming. He wanted to see whether the slanderer was acting from ignorance or from malice; by acting thus he generally attained what he wanted: slanderers, after their initial deep shame, became eulogists.

He was pitiless with notorious blockheads. He was infuriated by the customary saying, "Of course he makes mistakes, but his good intentions must be recognised . . ." He could not stand people who did the wrong thing with good intentions. What mattered to him was the result, not the "good intention". When people complained to him in a discussion about the shortcomings of several directors and intendants in the German Democratic Republic, he said: "Chuck them out!"

"But one can't simply put them on the street," said a "conciliator". "One can," said Brecht, "our street is not bad."

His understanding relationship with assistants and actors is well known. Of course there were rows, even "fearful rows". It would be petty-bourgeois idealisation not to mention them. But secretly I doubt that they were "genuine". In a "Katzgraben" rehearsal one point would simply not go right. Brecht continued rehearsing with a lot of patience, but I could not go on. He tapped my shoulder and said: "Don't say anything or there will be a genuine row. I'll make a theatre row and not get excited." He made the row. It worked. He smiled: "That's the way to do it."

If an actor spoke his text with undesirable pathos, or could not find the suitable gesture, Brecht utilised an astonishing method. He asked: "What is your dialect?" When he got the reply — South German, Rhenish, Saxon, he suggested that the passage should be delivered in the local dialect. The speaker became more relaxed and his gestures became looser and more natural. After a few rehearsals Brecht then returned to the Standard German text. Pathos and tension had generally disappeared.

If an actor thought that something was too difficult, impossible, Brecht encouraged him in Bavarian dialect: "You are an artist. For an arist there is nothing he can't do." By pushing an actor back into "staginess" he often achieved what he needed to carry out his complicated ideas.

People often say that actors — and artists in general — are like children. In my opinion, this naivety should not be destroyed. Brecht knew that without naivety there could be no great art, and agreed to all naive suggestions if they were not too extreme. In "Katzgraben" one actor insisted that he should come onstage with a piglet. Brecht did not laugh at him because of this really curious idea, but convinced him in several discussions that the piglet would disturb the performance.

He spoke to children like he spoke to adults, explaining to them quite naturally what he wanted of them, what he needed to achieve his idea of the play. He did not need to talk in childlike language because he expressed his ideas so clearly that children too could understand them.

In the last act of "Katzgraben" he wanted a scene of turbulence. At a village festival the children take a part. He watched what they had to offer and saw what effects they could produce. One little boy had to buy a bottle of lemonade at a stand, and drink it on the stage. The boy wanted the bottle to go pop when he opened it. It did not work right away. Brecht watched with interest. The assistant director became impatient. "Why are you taking such a long time with the bottle?" Brecht intervened: "Let him be. It's got to pop, and it ought to spurt too." The boy was happy because Brecht had understood him. From this time on the bottle popped at every rehearsal, and Brecht made sure that the props-man had a fresh "popping" bottle ready. If it was missing, the rehearsal was interrupted for it to be fetched.

In the *Stories of Herr Keuner* there is a passage which reveals that Herr Keuner did not like cats much; but he too showed the necessary respect for a cat which had done the work of stretching itself out to rest. This passage showed how well Herr Keuner had observed cats, although he did not like them much.

One evening I went to Brecht and found a black-and-white cat crawling round on his worktable. He licked Brecht's bread-and-butter and was very happy. "Just look, Herr Keuner and the cats," I said, in the tone in which we used to chaff each other. (He always asked me: "How's the horse?", referring to my weakness for horses.) Brecht became embarrassed. I noticed that he had abandoned his worktable so that the cat could have a free hand. He took the matter very seriously and delivered a long explanation why — you could not expel a cat at once and without more ado once it had turned up. Everything took time, and you had to take this and that into account. In the meantime the cat gnawed happily at his supper. On later visits I saw the cat again. It got cheekier, and my chaffing became more intensive; I must admit that it gave me pleasure to push Brecht, who always had such a ready wit, into embarrassed and theoretical cat discussions.

Once, it happened outside Berlin at Buckow, Young Pioneers paid a visit. Their teacher had coached them well, and sent them, equipped with unchildlike questions, into his workroom. "We are accomplishing a research project and making a scientific contribution. We are implementing the sounding of the shallows of the Buckow Lake . . ." The leader of the small group looked quickly at a piece of paper he had brought with him, and ground on in the style of a bad speaker: "We have discovered the fact that you are resident here. How is your life, Herr Brecht?"

"My life is hard," said Brecht shortly, although, as I mentioned before, he knew how to get along well with children; this answer was for the unfortunate teacher.

Brecht hated all routine, every "mechanisation" in the intellectual field, and when administrative measures and stupidity got the upper hand in the temples of the arts, he was not silent. We only have to recall his sudden intervention in the discussion about Ernst Barlach, his statement on the argument about Hanns Eisler's text for a Faust opera, and his poems about the Culture Commission. They should be re-read.

Some of us never learn, some learn slowly and thoroughly, others quickly and superficially, others so quickly that it just cannot be true. Those in the last category are the sinister prigs who are "in the picture" as soon as they have read the newspaper in the morning. Brecht preferred the category "slow and thorough". In my optimism it appears to me that many people in our Republic belong in this category. "How would it otherwise be possible that here, after five years, both praiseworthy and unpraiseworthy events have become history, in the full sense of the word? We are rightly proud of the praiseworthy things, and so we should laugh reflectively about the unpraiseworthy."

Brecht hated unreasonable administrative measures in artistic matters, but he was very accessible to properly based criticism. He observed his own work with sharp dialectic, shot at it with "whys" and "hows", made quick cuts, undertook changes without hesitation, and asked many friends and assistants for their opinions of what he had written.

"Katzgraben" reached the stage, but this did not end our collaboration. It developed into a working friendship. "Every friendship must produce something for both sides," he once said to me. As a result our frequent encounters were working discussions. We tested themes for their utility, and sought for opportunities to present, culturally, contemporary themes. In the last period he spoke often of his plan to write about Einstein and his "American tragedy". One evening he said: "How can you put the scene on the stage? Einstein writes a letter of the greatest importance to Roosevelt. How can that be dramatised? A real problem." Such questions naturally provoked the attempt to find answers.

Brecht followed world press every day. He promptly informed me with pleasure of every change of balance in favour of socialism, and he intervened at the right moment with one of his famous aphorisms when he knew that his words would be a weapon for the fighters for peace all over the world. Our discussions were often serious, particularly when they dealt with the possibility of a third world war; but in general both our talks and our work were cheerful, filled with that cheer which is indispensable for creative work.

I know no way of saying it better: since Brecht died I have never again laughed tears.

Caspar Neher
In Memory of My Friend
1957

A glance of agreement sufficed between us friends. We understood each other without many words, and for this reason it is particularly difficult for me to find words now that such glances are missing. I will report here on the last conversation I had with him. It was held in his Berlin apartment, shortly before I went to Salzburg in July. We spoke about his plans and my plans for the near future. He was sickly and drawn but he seemed to me to be on the mend, and not as though he would shortly be leaving us to descend to the realm of shadows — that realm which marked the end of his presence in the body, but which could not deprive us of his presence in the mind.

I had bought a copy of Wieland's translation of Cicero's letters, and told him of the custom of Hermae, bronze statues changed after a change of government. He wanted to use this in *Coriolanus*. I also told him about the custom of dressing in sackcloth and ashes when applying for a new post. In a note Wieland stated: *Itaque in luctu et squalore sum* — so am I in mourning and strewn with ashes — was an old custom at the funeral of friends and relatives. "There," he said, "over there," pointing to the cemetery near to his apartment, "you will soon be standing in *luctu et squalore*." With a laughing motion of his hand he passed on to speak about planning in old age. When we get to be sixty we shall have a lot behind us; we should drop some of those things which we still have to do today. Then we shall be able once again, as in our youth, to enjoy conversations, of which we get too little today. The time will come to quit the stage.

Several hours passed in conversation. We wanted to meet in Munich in August to spend a few weeks quietly somewhere. He had never shown such need of rest.

I could not know that things would happen differently. The frightful news hit us like lightning from a clear sky.

In my workroom I have a picture of his death mask. His face shows limitless peace. And although I cannot hear his voice I can hear his words; and a song by Ludwig Hölty, which he once recited to his friends, will not leave my mind.

> "Friends, when I'm dead,
> Hang up behind the altar the small harp,
> There on the wall where garlands glisten,
> Memories of girls now dead.
>
> The sexton, friendly, will show travellers
> The little harp with riband red
> That, firmly bound upon the harp,
> Trembles neath golden strings.
>
> Often, he says with bated breath,
> At eve the strings vibrate, like a bee's buzz —
> The children, charmed in from the churchyard,
> Heard it: and saw the garlands stir."

Vladimir Pozner
bb
1957

At the end of May last year I was sitting with Helene Weigel and her daughter in the tiny garden of their house in Berlin. The evening descended upon the single big tree, silencing its birds, and upon the neighbouring cemetery, the old Huguenot cemetery where Hegel is buried. I had come from Paris, bringing Brecht as a present a goat-milk cheese and a detective story. "Brecht will be very pleased," said Helene Weigel. When she spoke with her husband or referred to him she called him Brecht.

One year earlier in Paris, where *The Caucasian Chalk Circle* had struck like lightning, I had invited Brecht and his party to a small bar-restaurant on the Quais. Here they serve rare cheeses on a wooden plate; quite sufficient to make you forget Notre Dame across the way. Next door a bookshop, open in the evening, sold second-hand thrillers. That was where we started. Moving from shelf to shelf and even sifting the boxes on the floor, Brecht searched for detective stories in English; I had helped him to the extent of my knowledge, which was elementary compared to his; our wives had become impatient; finally he had purchased about thirty volumes. Now he was sitting comfortably on the terrace trying the cheeses, which were just as numerous as the books piled at his side; he had insisted on keeping them near to him.

The evening was mild, in front of us the street lights on the Petit Pont flickered, on the right you could guess the towers of Notre Dame. I drew Brecht's attention to a harmless looking goat cheese which was as sharp as dynamite. He tasted it and thanked me with a smile.

"Yes," he said thoughtfully, as though commenting simultaneously on the sharpness of the cheese, the mildness of the evening, and on the bells of Notre Dame and Saint Julien le Pauvre conversing over our heads.

He smiled without parting his lips, which gave him an embarrassed and almost shy look. His smile became more obvious, his small eyes began to gleam.

"I would like to exhibit this salver of cheeses in the foyer of my theatre," he said, "in order to show the Germans what culture is."

He was of course not thinking of the cheeses, but about the attractiveness of the way of life in the old Latin cultures, cultures from which Germany had never learned; he said it without sarcasm or malice but with regret. He spoke just as he wrote, in a completely direct manner, as a man who saw the world as a dialectician, and using the wonderful, hard, compact, tight-packed language peculiar to him. We used to call it laughingly a mixture of Bavarian, Latin, Chinese, and Brechtish; nobody could tame the German language as he did.

During this stay in Paris — his last — we met daily. In the great barn which the Théâtre Sarah-Bernhardt becomes in the absence of an audience his voice echoed strongly, while I translated the dark technical dialogue of the chief electrician of the Berliner Ensemble and his French colleagues. Brecht, who was quite capable of yelling, and who did not restrain himself, was extraordinarily polite to his collaborators.

One day I mobilised Brecht and Helene Weigel together with the other actors, the chief electrician and the rest of the technicians for a reportage for "l'Humanité-Dimanche". Brecht subjected himself more with discipline than patience to the orders of the photographer: vexation lent him a sad appearance.

With regard to photographs Brecht was demanding, and checked them carefully before permitting their publication. He obviously had an even more definite idea of his physical appearance than most people, and turned down every photo which did not fit his image. If you were to study the photographs which he approved, and compare them to those which he rejected, it might be possible to reconstruct Brecht's picture of himself as he liked himself; or, we may assume, as he least disliked himself. All of us react in the same way. When I discussed the subject with him one day he smiled and said: "I know that I look stupid, but why should I admit it to others?"

He looked carefully at the pictures made by the photographer from "l'Humanité" before selecting those which he approved. I looked at the others: they looked like him — not more and not less.

In addition there were the journalists, not very many of them. Brecht often asked me to translate; we had the bad habit that every now and then we discussed things flippantly — in German — while the visitor waited for the answer to his serious question.

"Yes," Brecht would say with his shy smile, as though he was answering after long meditation, "what could we tell him?"

My suggestion was generally lacking in seriousness; led astray by this, Brecht assessed the suggestion in all possible contexts, producing ten different answers, one more preposterous than the other. I had to call him to order: "He's waiting."

At once he put his ideas precisely in words, with the help of his politeness, while the pen of the interviewer raced over the paper.

At noon we met again in the restaurant on the Boulevard Sébastopol, where the guests from Berlin usually took their meals. "I thought that 'Parmentier' was 'Parmesan'," said Brecht, "and now I have got to eat a potato cake."

In the evenings we made ourselves comfortable on the terrace of the café next to the theatre and waited for the performance to end. The crowd overflowed the pavement onto the road, and amongst them there was not a soul who knew the man with the fringed hair, who in the fifteenth century might have stood model for any early painter, for any Augsburg master, this peasant with his jacket buttoned to the neck; not a soul who knew that he was a poet of genius, the creator of myths, of sagas, of the entire folklore of an unknown people which had certainly never existed, but which was not dissimilar to the German people.

That was one year ago, and in the meantime I had visited Berlin several times. The hotel in which I stayed was a five minutes walk from Brecht's home. You just needed to lift the phone. This time I did not even phone. To the right of the door were two bell-pushes, one marked "BB" and the other "HWB". Upstairs there was no light. I pressed the downstairs button.

"Barbara," said Helene Weigel, "go and see if Brecht is still up and if somebody can come up to say hello."

She came back a moment later.

"Daddy has turned out the light," she said. "He'll be asleep: he felt poorly."

Brecht had been feeling poorly for some time. His temperature stayed above normal, sometimes a bit more, sometimes a bit less. He had consulted the best doctors in Berlin. The specialists had found something wrong with his kidneys, and something with his heart; they had ordered him a course of treatment, to which he submitted with discipline. But the temperature withstood the injections, and the exhaustion did too.

The timing was inconvenient. Brecht was in the midst of rehearsals for the greatest of his plays, *The Life of Galileo*. He had had to interrupt this work. His wife was worried, but not unduly; the doctors had said there was no reason for alarm. A nurse came every evening to spend the night upstairs, but this was because Brecht slept quite alone up there. On that evening we told each other stories in the balmy little garden; we took care not to make much noise.

On the day after my visit Brecht went for two days to his

house at Buckow, not far from Berlin. His nights were better there, and his temperature fell, though not to the normal level. He extended his stay in the country. I left Berlin without seeing him again, without guessing that he would soon rest near Hegel in the old Huguenot cemetery. During my previous visit I had spoken to him for the last time, and that right in the middle of a rehearsal of *Galileo*.

We had got to know each other fifteen years earlier in Hollywood. In this luxury mining town, the cinema was our common gold mine. We even wrote a film script jointly, together with a friend. Every morning we met in the roomy house of this untamable woman; the house where Eisenstein had lived, where Greta Garbo picked up her letters, where Charlie Chaplin was a frequent guest. We lolled in the only drawing room in Hollywood in which the armchairs were worn and comfortable, and invented our story aloud. It played in France during the liberation struggle, with flashbacks to the past. France was ten thousand kilometres away; our only sources of information were our memories and our love for France. It is perhaps too much to speak of Brecht's "love" for France. I know that he loved the writers, the artists and the revolutions of France. He devoted two plays to France: the Paris Commune was the subject of the first, and the other brought to the stage a Joan of Arc from the last war. In any case it appeared to me that our script *The Silent Witness*, for which Brecht had the idea, and which I have half forgotten today, accorded with the facts, and was worth relating. This was a double illusion in a town which offered good prospects for the winner of a Beautiful Bust contest, but condemned to idleness actresses like Helene Weigel and Ludmilla Pitoëff.

With ashtrays overflowing between us, we argued bitterly. Our hostess, the most generous, the most passionate, the most red-headed of all women, burst out unceasingly. She wanted to know all the circumstances of each psychological step, of every dramatic clash.

"But what about this figure?" she interrupted obstinately

for the tenth time. "We don't know her yet, she must be introduced first."

"She will be explained when she is needed for the action, not before," said Brecht, keeping his control with an effort.

"Why?" she shouted.

Shaking with fury he raised his voice: "And when she is no longer needed, then she will no longer be mentioned."

With her beautiful arms stretched in the air, with her fighting red hair, looking much like the "Marseillaise" by François Rude, she insisted: "Why? I want to know why."

"Because I said so. That is enough," Brecht shouted. Stubbing his cigar in the ashtray he set a full stop to the discussion.

We always reached agreement, and after the passions had cooled I dictated to the secretary the new scene.

"Above all," said Brecht, with the charitable smile of the short-sighted, as he lighted his cigar again, "we must never forget for one moment that we are writing this script in order to sell it."

"That's true," said our hostess with a throaty laugh, "we must put ourselves in the shoes of the producers."

"I am putting myself in their shoes," said Brecht modestly.

I could not well imagine Brecht as the small and heated Jack Warner, the Kentucky Colonel; nor as the oily Louis B. Mayer, at that time the almighty boss of Metro-Goldwyn-Mayer. I was probably right. Nobody wanted our script, which Hollywood regarded as too realistic or too romantic, probably both. Somewhere I still have a copy, typed up in the style known only between Burbank and Culver City.

We bore our failure with stoicism, though it is always disappointing not to draw the winning ticket. Cinema had become the least of our worries; the narrow horizons of Hollywood had just burst.

I left first. Brecht only managed to leave the United States at the end of 1947. At that time this was no easy undertaking for a German anti-fascist who wanted to travel to the zone occupied by the Red Army. It may be assumed that the allies, already the "western" allies, did nothing to facilitate such a journey.

But the Committee on Un-American Activities, for its part, did everything in its power to drag Brecht into the case of the Hollywood Ten. Let us recall the facts: they were trying to prove that the "Reds" were spreading their ideas in the United States by way of the cinema screen, and had formed cells in the studios. This was probably the first time that anybody ever mentioned ideas in connection with American cinema. The newspapers screamed about conspiracies, and every conspiracy naturally implies aliens. Brecht lived in Hollywood, and on the list of allegedly "hostile" witnesses — hostile to the Committee — he was among the second ten.

He appeared before the Committee, which was chaired by the Honorable J. Parnell Thomas (or rather the ex-Honorable, for he had already committed his embezzlements, but not yet been sent to prison for them). The record of Brecht's testimony is one of the most astounding documents of that period. As somebody said, it was as if apes had taken to examining the biologist.

Brecht did not refuse to speak about politics, but said that the arts interested him more. In order to change the subject, without interrupting the context, a sentence sufficed. The Committee had some difficulty in bringing him back to the only theme in which it was interested.

"Yes," said Brecht in a dragging voice, putting into this word, as he so well could, simultaneously respect for his partners, understanding for their point of view, and complete disagreement on his part.

And he crowned the whole performance with a lecture on the old Japanese theatre, to which the members of the Committee listened with open mouths, before they realised what they had let themselves in for, and sent the burdensome witness packing.

Brecht utilised this chance to take the first available plane for Europe; he had booked a seat in advance. He left the

New World as he had left the Old World some years earlier; the tragedy was repeated, but it had become a farce.

In Berlin tragedy and farce were inextricably mixed. After Brecht's return I had the opportunity to visit Berlin about ten times, possibly more. More than once we walked with him through the city, or what remained of it, and this was not very much. In the ruins elderly women gleaned the less damaged bricks, which they carefully cleaned before piling them. In the bare skeletons of buildings the central-heating pipes climbed the walls and stretched their radiators into the air like giant accordions.

I can still see Brecht stopping in front of a large abandoned building in the Friedrich Strasse: the name of the building "House of Technology" still hung over the grand portals, surrounded by innumerable broken windows and twisted girders. This House of Technology was extremely comical because of the way in which it had been treated by technology. We stood there for at least five minutes admiring it and exchanging jests. Brecht's cracks could be biting.

Sometimes we stood in front of shopwindows displaying horrible mauve undergarments decorated with extraordinary ecru lace, which the state-owned stores offered at that time to the German public. Brecht spoke about the lasting nature of petty-bourgeois taste, and about the hunger for abundance experienced by a class which comes to power; moderation only appears slowly.

Amidst the ruins he had begun to build up the best theatre in Europe. The government had provided him with a huge barn in the Reinhardt Strasse, formerly used as a shooting range. Those who built it had not provided for artillery fire, however, and the shells and bombs of the Second World War had not spared the building. Patched up provisionally, it now had some resemblance to Baron Münchhausen's horse, torn in two by a cannon ball.

There Brecht held his rehearsals, surrounded by his small staff, various pupils and friends living in Berlin or paying a visit. I have never seen a director who made so little attempt to guard his secrets; here, as later in the Theater am Schiffbauerdamm, anybody could walk in who wanted to. The porters — if there were any porters — were so discreet that I never noticed them. You opened a few doors and found yourself in the auditorium. Scattered through the dim hall, men and women followed the rehearsal. Brecht turned round, gave you a smile, waved you to a seat, went on with his work.

Every time I went to Berlin I met Brecht: as chance had it we worked together more than once.

We first co-operated on Joris Ivens' film, "Song of the Rivers", for which I wrote the script, and for which Brecht had agreed to write the songs. After a day in and around the cutting-rooms I spoke with him in the evening about the songs. He puffed at his cigar, which was out more often than it was lighted, smiled as though in apology, and said mildly: "Yes ... well what could we say?" He had agreed to write a song for each river, and now he was suffering.

"Do we have to make the rivers speak?" he asked himself aloud.

"Perhaps," I suggested, "the people who live on the banks."

He lit his cigar once again.

"The workers of the country through which the river flows," he considered, "or the workers of all countries, who are today the masters of all rivers or will become the masters?"

When I visited him two days later he took from his desk a yellow sheet of paper, typed without capitals.

"Do you think this will do?" he asked, and read me the *Song of the Nile*. "For the moment that is all," he said smilingly, as though in apology.

He lit his cigar again.

"I am still worried about the rhymes," he said.

Down the margin of the paper there was a narrow handwritten column: a selection of rhymes.

Then Shostakovich arrived in Berlin. He was due to write the music for the film. One evening he visited Brecht together with Ivens and myself.

There was a resemblance between the two which was not simply confined to the similarity of their hair styles. One spoke Russian and the other German, and the interpreter had difficulty in following.

"I am pleased to be working with you," said Brecht, "and I am sure that you will write a fine song."

"One never knows," said Shostakovich, "I managed it once with *Nas utro vstrechayet prokhladnoi*, but it is a matter of luck. But I shall do my best, because I know that you write good texts."

"That is a matter of luck," said Brecht. "What has happened is that a number of my songs have come out right; that is all. It is impossible to tell in advance. Luckily your music will be there."

"It's difficult," said Shostakovich with a doubtful expression.

"It's very difficult," said Brecht.

And they were definitely not being coy. Brecht was unassuming though not unexacting, and listened, mostly in silence, to any criticism.

"Yes," he said with a small smile, "yes."

But I also heard him say one day: "There are only two directors in the world."

The other was Chaplin.

And when I reproached him for his adaptation of "Don Juan" by Molière, he replied quite seriously: "But it was adapted by Brecht."

The two small letters — bb — which he so often used as his signature accorded both with his modesty and his pride.

A film studio in Vienna decided to put *Puntila and His Servant Matti* on the screen, and Brecht insisted that I should write the film version. I went to Berlin to visit him.

In his home in the Chaussee Strasse, into which he had

just moved, we started to work as we had done ten years earlier in Hollywood. He was waiting for me every morning at nine, already shaved and in his grey jacket. (You might have thought it was always the same one; one day I met a young actress from the Berliner Ensemble at the tailor's, with the famous jacket on her arm: "Herr Brecht wants you to make one just like this," she said.) Brecht was surrounded by a jumble of curiously shaped and un-matched armchairs, very small tables, a tiny harmonium, a portable typewriter. Half-smoked cigars lay around on pewter plates; on the walls there were an engraving, Chinese masks, and two small old photos, one of Marx when his beard was still black, and the other of a very young Engels. All the horizontal planes disappeared under a chaos of paper: music, manuscripts, letters, posters, books. Through the window you could see the tiny garden, the tree in which the black-birds piped, and the Huguenot cemetery beyond.

"Hegel is buried down there," Brecht told me on the very first day, and I resolved to go there one day.

We sat opposite one another and talked. Once again it was a case of knocking together a script. With a rapid-fire exchange of jokes we got to work. I don't know if the jokes were good, but we never stopped laughing: I have never worked so merrily. Brecht loved laughing and making people laugh; he laughed in small jerks which changed into a roar when new jokes arrived; red from hilarity he rocked backwards and forwards and clutched his thighs with both hands.

We were often interrupted by the telephone bell. Brecht waited for a short while, hoping for a miracle; a stranger who would get discouraged and hang up. But the stranger never hung up. Brecht excused himself and went to pick up the phone: because of his extreme courtesy he always apologised.

The telephone stood in his bedroom, a sort of monkish cell with only space for his bed and a desk disappearing under its load of detective stories. After a moment Brecht returned; while answering the caller he had thought of a new joke. A little later a snack was brought in: sandwiches and tea.

"In the thirty years in which Puntila has not seen her," Brecht said, speaking of one of our figures, "she has not grown younger."

We began to laugh again, and the telephone again started to ring. It might be the head of the government, or one of Brecht's assistants arriving from the provinces, a Dutch poet who had lost his way in Berlin, or dear old Hanns Eisler. For all of them Brecht felt curiously responsible, particularly for his country and his people; for those who had died in the war and the camps, and still more for the living.

I visited him when he returned from Dresden; the German peace movement had just commemorated the tenth anniversary of the destruction of Dresden during the war.

Brecht had taken there the signatures to his appeal addressed to the intellectuals of the German Democratic Republic.

"Something like this has never before happened," said Brecht. "People who have never before given their signatures have joined us. Some of them scissored the appeal out of the newspaper, stuck it on a piece of paper, and signed it; others wrote it out or typed it out and circulated it amongst friends and acquaintances. The students went from lecture room to lecture room, from laboratory to laboratory. An actor mobilised an entire theatre, and a musician an entire orchestra."

Inside two months about four-fifths of the intellectuals of the country had signed this appeal protesting against the Paris Treaties [re-arming the Federal Republic of Germany, trans.]. I asked why.

"Why?" Brecht repeated, lighting his cigar again. "Because the partitioning of the country is intolerable. We all — all — have relatives on the other side. And also because people are afraid of atomic war."

That evening I read in my hotel room for the first time the few lines which Brecht had written two years earlier against German re-armament:

Great Carthage waged three wars. After the first it was still mighty. After the second it was still habitable. After the third it was not to be found.

I picked up the phone, dialled Brecht's number and let it ring. When I heard his voice I simply asked (I knew the answer with certainty, but I wanted to hear it from his mouth): "What is Carthage?"

"Carthage," said Brecht firmly, "is Germany."

He was never untrue to this feeling of responsibility. I recall the day on which Rafael Alberti asked me to introduce him to Brecht. Since they lacked a common language they grasped each other's hands for a long time. They stood there and looked at each other smilingly, the Spaniard with the broad shoulders and the greying hair with a big sunny smile, and the German with his half-embarrassed, half-shy smile. Finally Brecht spoke.

"Ask him," he said to me, "whether he has a decent place to stay in Berlin."

"Yes," said Alberti.

"Ask him," said Brecht, "whether his room is nice and warm."

That happened last year during the German Writers' Congress, and the next day I went to a rehearsal of *Galileo*. Brecht had asked me to come to the theatre to record on tape several sentences in French which occurred in the play and which he needed for his work. Terrified, I stood in front of the microphone under Ernst Busch's critical eye and Brecht said: "Very good, very good. Now repeat it once again, but more slowly and louder."

And without saying the words he showed me — as he showed his actors — the tone, the rhythm, the strength, the whole sound-curve of the sentences I had to say.

That was work, and he was serious. Immediately afterwards he told me that with a voice like mine I should have become a cardinal, all appearances to the contrary.

I met him again in the corridor of the theatre, where he had come to see me out. He shook my hand and bowed slightly as was his habit, as he had probably learned to do as a child.

"At least a cardinal," he said.

That was the last time I heard his voice. I saw him once more. A few days later, walking along his street, I saw him from afar at the wheel of a very old open car. He was sitting very straight, his cap was flat upon his head, a dead cigar was clenched between his teeth. Without thinking that one should never put anything off, I resolved to tell him next time we met of the figure that I had seen, a snapshot which seemed to have escaped from one of those old Chaplin comedies which made Brecht laugh so much.

P. S. Berlin, November 27th. I tell the driver he should take me to the Huguenot cemetery in the Chaussee Strasse.

"There where Brecht is buried?" he asks.

The skies are grey, the trees bare. Between the graves, so many of which bear old French family names, preceded by a long row of old-fashioned Christian names, men and women are sweeping up the dead leaves, laying pine branches at the foot of stone crosses. I go once, and then again, round the whole graveyard without finding anything.

A woman approaches. "You are looking for Herr Brecht?" She points to a wall in the background.

"He lies buried on the other side. You have to go out into the street, keep left, and take the first entrance on the left."

The gate is half open. I go along the path which runs past Brecht's house, under his window, and to a second cemetery. I wander vainly among the graves, read the names, but fail to find the one I seek. I ask a woman to help me. "That's difficult to find," she says, "there's no inscription on it or anything." She gestures for me to follow her. She walks slowly, a Berlin housewife, in the fifties, heavy, a black hat, a grey raincoat.

She points to a broad carpet of pine branches against the red bricks of the wall, where a very small birch tree grows. Next to it lies Doctor Emil Osann "born on May 25th 1787, died on January 11th 1842." Opposite, a little further away, lies Marie Hegel, née von Tucher, the wife of Georg Wilhelm Hegel, between her husband and Johann Gottlieb Fichte. If you look up you can see the bomb-pocked grey wall of the house in which Brecht lived.

"There," said the woman. "Herr Brecht. It was his wish that nothing should be written on his grave."

She does not know that the gravestone is not yet ready. Thus do legends arise.

Anna Seghers
Brecht

1957

Brecht once told me that I must never write a single sentence negligently. I must bear the responsibility for every sentence. Not just for the sense. For every word and every comma. You should not leave a single sentence before checking it again and again.

This is true. I think of his advice whatever I write. But I do not always follow it. Even now, writing these lines, I am not following it. But Brecht is the only person who would understand why I am writing too quickly and too briefly about him. He would understand that I have to write about him between two pieces of work. He liked the sentence: Life is densely occupied.

But no day passes for me, I learn of no event, whether great or quite small, when I do not think: Brecht ought to write about it. However much he may have left, I feel sad about the realities which now stream uninterruptedly over his grave, and can no longer be described by him. I want to ask his advice, and he no longer answers; I want to praise him, and he is no longer pleased; I want to reprimand him, and he is no longer annoyed; I want to show him something special, and he is no longer astonished; I want to tell him something funny, and he no longer laughs. He was so entirely us; he belonged to us so completely. Clearing rubble out of brains. Building. I recall that he once said to me: "Don't go all round the house when you want to go to the garden; it doesn't disturb me, even if I'm working, if people go through my room."

Nobody is as unassuming as he was.

Johannes R. Becher

Summer Lament

I

A lilac bush blossomed in May,
Ballooning
Like a hill of blue
Beside the tender
Bloom of sloe . . .

And once again the boats
Glide silent as a dream.
Heavens and lake are one.
An unexpected summer,
But — lacking you.

I feel anxiety
When August comes.
For it was in this month
You left us,
Moving away from Buckow,
You left to us the sorrow,
Alone.

Never again my drive from Saarow to Buckow.
For what is now the sense
In journeying this road?

Perhaps I shall meet you elsewhere?

But perhaps
You have passed in eternity
Into me too,
And I must only seek you here
To find you?

2

But there is also envy,
Flattery,
Suspicion,
Persecution,
Not solely by enemies . . .
A mixed choir singing at his grave

Kyrie eleison!
Blessed be Brecht!

3

August is nearing

Will it always be for me
A month of despairing remembrance?

A shattering message:
Bert is gone . . .

Perilous the message for me also.
We all are mortally wounded,
Whether admitting it or not.

August is nearing

The hymnic month,
In the passion of its glow,
Reeling with lust
Drunk with summer joy
Wonderful in its frenzy
Revelling
In heavy colours —

Joyously the song of life rings out,
In mourning too,
Giving you thanks.

August is nearing.

1958

Günter Kunert
Memories of Bertolt B.

1962–63

Braying laughter. Unrhythmic irregular movements of his round head: tension before the constant start. High pressure in the grey costume; the only safety valve: the cigar. Bright eyes, strong words: shit the weakest. Two leather loafers which go to and fro with him. Fervently believing nothing. Fabulating. Of generous miserliness. Continuance only of change is allowed by this last saint of doubt, ascetic sybarite, and prophet of the science of art and the art of knowledge. Sometimes: in a tiny chair which could rock, near to his earth, low on the wooden floor; the others, we, on raised seats. And we looked up to him. And he was no longer there.

Konstantin Fedin
Bertolt Brecht
1956

Bertolt Brecht's death is a hard blow for the arts. The departure of this bold artist and seeker has torn a gap in the ranks of German theatre, a gap which nobody can fill. The international theatre will feel bitterly this unexpected loss.

As a dramatist and poet Brecht was the master of social themes. As a director he was the master of social theatre. His work as a dramatist and as a director belonged together.

The agreement between the inspiration of the writer and the temperament of the director was governed by the aim which he had chosen for himself, once and for all — to create the drama of the contemporary social struggle. Historic and contemporary events had the same value for him, if they expressed the struggle between the classes. He was never frightened of politics in art. On the contrary, he dealt with politics as a perfectly normal subject for art. He knew that if he deprived the play of political coloration he would rob his art of its social influence.

Naturally the Brecht of the 1920s differs from the Brecht of our day, judged from the content of his dramatic works. His school was an epoch of upheavals, wars and revolutions. He did not fear to attend this school, and the straightforwardness of his solution in terms of ideas was no less bold than his artistic concepts, the originality of which cost him many struggles.

The critics will certainly have to differentiate between three periods in Brecht's artistic work. During the Weimar Republic he fought untiringly against absolutism and philistinism. During his years of exile he was a dauntless enemy of Hitlerite fascism. Then he became a real and true poet of the German Democratic Republic, born out of the Second World War. In his artistic production all three stages are generously represented.

But what was Brecht's unique quality as the head of a theatre?

Life on the stage was for Brecht that plankton which fed and nourished his untiring experiments as a writer.

His workroom was both the starting point and the continuation of events on the stage. The element of co-operation governed his entire work. He never implemented as an individual his discoveries, his inventions; he checked them, altered them, changed them and supplemented them with the help of his friends — actors, painters, directors, musicians, writers. I had the opportunity more than once to observe Brecht when he was working on a new play or preparing a new performance. He was always waiting for somebody, somebody was on the way, or he was already surrounded by assistants and talking to somebody, a manuscript before him, with crossed-out pieces of paper on all sides.

I was astonished by the size and the emptiness of his workroom outside the city. Isolated tables and chairs stood in various corners. Brecht said:

"They are for my assistants. We want to see as well as we can what we are preparing for the stage; for that reason we need a lot of room."

Work as a playwright was for him simultaneously work as a director. The play itself included the coming staging, and only the team could see clearly in advance this staging from the manuscript. Thus the workroom of Brecht the dramatist became a laboratory with many assistants.

What did the stage mean for him when the play became converted into a performance? It became an area of co-operation with the audience. The theatre team had checked its work on the spectator before the production took the stage. The bridge between the stage and the auditorium had been built before the audience took their seats.

And even more: the spectators were drawn into the work of the dramatist. Only a short while ago Brecht told me how he had gradually been able to interest the farmers of a co-operative farm in a play which was taking shape; on their farm a dam was being built. The farmers were first invited to watch a rehearsal; they began to question various arguments and episodes, and Brecht spurred them on with the question: "And what does it look like at your place?" They finally reached the stage at which the theatre went to the village and observed their lives. Brecht asked the farmers' advice on how to change the episodes; and as a result he and his troupe worked on the play together with the farmer-spectators. Brecht told me, with his slightly sly smile:

"They believed that they were simply giving us some help. In fact, without noticing it, they were helping their co-operative. They began to have the slightly embarrassing feeling that a play was being written about them, and actors were performing it, but they were not getting on very well with the construction of the dam in their village. The only thing to be done was to get on with the dam ... So we see that art can influence life in this way too."

Such a method of work is characteristic for his really bold attempts to achieve a co-operation between the playwright, the actor and the audience in creating a new form of stage art. Theatrical experts and critics speak so often of Brecht's individualism; but in fact this "individualist" constructs the whole of his activity upon the basis of a broad and living collaboration with the mass of the various collective groups. He was never deaf to the "alien" voice of an adviser; on the contrary he listened with attention and voluntarily surrounded himself with people who gave him advice.

Bertolt Brecht had dreamed of showing his theatre to the Soviet spectator. It is a cause for great sorrow that now that a tour has been arranged for his troupe, he himself will not be able to hear the music and words, and to see the colours of the performance of his plays on the Moscow stage.

But his theatre, his dramatic work, his poems, his works on theory and instruction — everything that is left behind by this seeker, this outstanding, powerful talent — will naturally persist and live on.

Käthe Rülicke - Weiler
"Since then
the World has Hope"
1968

Brecht in the Soviet Union

> *It would be quite wrong for socialists to believe that they should hide their light under a bushel, perhaps because it might dazzle. It may dazzle, because it is night. What the socialists must display is the way out. If somebody shows how to dominate a situation, is he therefore domineering? And if the answer is yes, then he should be domineering!*

In May 1955 the "International Lenin Prize for Strengthening Peace between the Peoples" was awarded to Brecht in the Kremlin in Moscow. Brecht noted: "It is the extraordinary custom of the Soviet Union, this most extraordinary state, to award to several people every year a prize for the efforts they have made for world peace. Such a prize seems to me the highest and most desirable prize which could be awarded today."

In fact the award of this prize meant much to Brecht. His works had only just begun to be published in the Soviet Union. A volume *Poems and Prose* had been published there in German in 1953, but the preface distorted rather than explained Brecht's intentions, and particularly his views on the theatre. It is true that Dymshitz and Motylova had been publishing essays on Brecht since the beginning of the 1950s, but his plays had not been staged since Tairov's somewhat unsuccessful *Threepenny Opera* in Moscow in 1930. At the same time Brecht was well aware that his Soviet friends had played a decisive part in helping to establish the Berliner Ensemble, particularly Lieutenant Colonel Alexander Dymschitz, at that time cultural officer of the Soviet Military Administration, today professor for dramaturgy at the Moscow Film Institute, translator of *The Days of the Commune*, and author of many articles on Brecht and other German writers.

Writing about the period after the October Revolution, Brecht had noted: "The young Soviet Government, hard-pressed from within and without, showed touching care for the theatre amidst war and starvation. Help was given in the form of coal, special rations, urgent tasks." And turning to the present, Brecht continued: "This was repeated 25 years later when the Soviet Commandant in conquered Berlin gave orders, in the very first days, that the theatres which Hitler had closed should be re-opened. The enemy, defeated with such difficulty, was invited to the theatre. The first things the victors did were to supply bread, ensure water supplies, and open the theatres."

New friends were added to the old ones, just as Brecht's relationship with the first socialist state, dating back decades, was reflected in new poems on the Soviet Union. In 1929, the year in which he wrote the poem *The Vanished Fame of the Great City of New York*, Brecht wrote his famous *The Carpet-weavers of Kuyan Bulak Honour Lenin*, together with other poems, which he called *Stories from the Revolution*.

In the time of growing confusion over the whole planet
We await the second plan
Of the first communist commonwealth

wrote Brecht in his poems *Waiting for the Second Five-Year Plan* and *The International*, praising the organisation of the new society.

At a time when the capitalist propaganda campaign against the young Soviet state was on the increase, Brecht studied Lenin's works "State and Revolution", "Imperialism as the Highest Stage of Capitalism", and "Two Tactics for

Social Democracy in the Democratic Revolution", which were published in German from 1927 on, and which formed part of Brecht's reference library. According to Tretyakov, Brecht liked to read aloud with enormous enthusiasm from Lenin's works, as other writers read Cicero and Virgil.

Brecht, who had approached Marxism through the tasks set him by his plays, became a friend of the Soviet Union at a period when the policy of the Communist Party of Germany was awakening a growing echo. In his *Ballad of the Steel Helmets* he joined in the protest action against the rally planned for May 1927 by the reactionary militarist organisation "Stahlhelm" (steel helmet). The protest had been called for by Ernst Thälmann at the 11th Party Congress of the Communist Party of Germany. In this poem, published in the Communist satirical magazine "Der Knüppel", to which Brecht had been giving his political poems since 1926, he paid tribute to the October Revolution and the historic role of the Soviet Union:

> *Useless were helmets and cannons*
> *And the White battalions*
> *Failed to reach Leningrad.*
>
> *Never will helmets and cannons,*
> *Never will White battalions,*
> *Hold back history's wheel.*

The sympathies of many left-wing middle-class writers had been won by the Leninist mass policy pursued by the Communist Party of Germany after the 10th Congress in 1925, and by the "Red Cultural Fighting Front" closely allied with the class struggle. The process of differentiation was speeded up by the growing sharpening of economic contradictions, and by the resultant political struggles. First Johannes R. Becher, Erich Weinert and Friedrich Wolf, and then Anna Seghers, Ludwig Renn, Egon Erwin Kisch joined the "League of Proletarian-Revolutionary Writers". Brecht, increasingly in sympathy with the policies of the

Communist Parties of Germany and the Soviet Union, aligned himself with Communism first with poems, and then in 1930 with his play *The Measures Taken*.

Sternberg reports: "His sympathies were for the Communist Party; he was not uncritical, but held the view that its errors were correctable." Brecht attended lectures at MASCH (Marxist Workers' School) in Neukölln, Berlin, where Hermann Duncker was his teacher.

The Measures Taken includes the first of Brecht's "songs of praise" which have since become famous and are still applicable today: *"Praise for the Party, Praise for the Soviet Union* and *Praise for Illegal Work.* The *Cantata on Lenin's Death* includes the *Praise for the Revolutionary,* which he then incorporated in *The Mother,* the play for which he also wrote *Praise for Learning* and *Praise for Communism.*

> *The individual can be destroyed,*
> *But the Party cannot be destroyed.*

In these words Brecht summed up the necessity for the fighting solidarity of the working class and its advance detachment. Brecht's children's poem *The Three Soldiers* with illustrations by George Grosz was also published at this time; this work, with which he wished to awaken young people against the injustice done to the poor, has been unjustly disregarded.

In the 1920s Brecht had already made friends with Soviet artists, for instance Sergei Tretyakov. Tretyakov was one of the first to recognise Brecht's importance. He popularised him in the Soviet Union, and wrote a long article about his plays; later, in 1947, when Brecht had to appear before the Committee on Un-American Activities, this article was produced as incriminating evidence.

In 1930 Brecht was greatly impressed by the guest performances given by Meyerhold in Berlin. He had discovered a theatre which devoted itself to the fulfilment of political tasks. This theatre showed society as something governed by class struggle, and attempted to express this by artistic means — openly displaying itself as "theatre", by the groupings, the impressive gestures of the actors, social characterisation, the presentation of work processes, and so on. Young Soviet art exerted upon Brecht an influence which was decisive for his ties with contemporary art. This influence differed from other influences — for instance Elizabethan theatre, the theatre of Sturm und Drang, the theatres of other times and other lands — since it did not call first of all for contradiction; in contemporary Germany it could only be compared with the theatre of Piscator or with proletarian "Agitprop" art. Brecht was able to adopt directly the achievements of Soviet art, and extend them in his theatrical work, naturally taking into consideration social developments in Germany and the tasks which these posed.

After Meyerhold's guest performances Brecht wrote:

"It was rather depressing to read German theatre critics on Meyerhold. Impression-collectors appear uninterested in the historical position which Meyerhold's experiments hold in the attempts to achieve a great and rational theatre. For such people it is a matter of indifference that here all concepts have been adjusted, a matter of indifference that we are presented here with a real theory about the social function of the theatre . . ."

"The presentation of the British in China caused almost the most resentment here. In 'Roar, China!' the Russians show too little interest in the possible nice side of the British in their private lives. It is as though it would be necessary to show, in a play about King Attila's bloody deeds, how fond he was of children."

Brecht also acknowledged the influence upon his work of Eisenstein and Mayakovsky, who also identified themselves with the revolution. With regard to play structure Eisenstein probably influenced Brecht most. Eisenstein who, as he wrote, "always combined creative work with analytical work," organised the artistic effect with a view to the audience, just as Brecht did.

Brecht saw Eisenstein's film, "Armoured Cruiser Potemkin", just at the time when he was attempting to derive the construction of the plot from the laws of development of reality in his preparatory work for *Saint Joan of the Stockyards,* and "Potemkin" influenced not only this play but even more *The Mother.* The dialectical confrontation of contradictory actions, commenting upon each other and driving each other forward in *The Mother,* is constructed in a similar manner to that used in Eisenstein's film, in which class antagonism is the ruling element: on one hand the state power, personified by the officers' clique and the soldiers which they command; and on the other hand the revolutionary sailors and the masses who give them support. In *The Mother* Brecht mixed the individual story of Pelegea Vlassova with the story of the Party group which, generalising the social message, confront her as chorus.

In Eisenstein's films the events are not simply arranged in accordance with the laws of the materialist dialectic, but proletarian partisanship becomes the montage principle, governing selection, close-ups, details. Eisenstein stated that "montage-adjusted thought is one of the common features of all branches of art" which border upon literature, and Brecht found this feature in the works of Mayakovsky too. Mayakovsky's lines of poetry have a gestic content just as Brecht's rhymeless rhythms have. Mayakovsky's plays (Brecht knew the "Mysterium Buffo" at an early date) are scenes of action for the class struggle. But alienation also belongs to Mayakovsky's working principles; he had a great fancy for contradictory situations and contents, and for verbal montage. Like Brecht, Mayakovsky presents to the audience a confrontation between well-known situations and the present — in "Mysterium Buffo" he does this with scenes from the Bible. The works of both men are intended to provoke productivity and to encourage a reconstruction of society.

In Soviet left-wing art Brecht found models in whose works the *unity of art and politics* had been implemented, a principle at which he aimed in his own works.

Natalia Rosenel, the wife of Anatoli V. Lunacharsky, the first Soviet People's Commissar for Education, has described Brecht's meetings with Lunacharsky in 1928, 1931 and 1933. She notes that Brecht was well informed about everything new in Soviet theatre, and that he followed with interest the plays and performances. Assia Lazis, who had helped Brecht in 1923 in staging *The Life of Edward II of England* at the Munich Kammerspiele Theatre, and who had been his first informant on developments in the Soviet Union, has reported the interest with which he followed at that time developments there.

Lunacharsky and Brecht had become acquainted at evenings arranged by VOKS, the "Society of Friends of Soviet Russia" and at receptions in the Soviet Embassy, before Lunacharsky saw *The Threepenny Opera* and got to know Brecht's plays. Natalia Rosenel recalls how in January 1933 theatre people met Lunacharsky in Brecht's apartment and discussed what would await left intellectuals if Hitler came to power: emigration, illegality, destruction. She quotes what Lunacharsky said: " 'Even in emigration or living illegally you can continue the fight ... Remember us and the Russian Bolsheviks. Neither abroad in emigration nor in Siberian banishment did we lay aside our weapons. We knew that we would win. When I was in emigration in Switzerland I studied schools, the educational system. I knew that as soon as the revolution had been victorious I would have to work in the educational field: so I prepared myself for this.' Then he turned to Brecht: 'Brecht, you for instance. You will write your plays, although for the time being nobody will stage them; but in a few years, I am quite sure, there will be a Brecht theatre in Berlin, in which you will be author, director, and perhaps even actor!' ... And Anatoli Lunacharsky raised his glass and said: 'Long live Brecht's theatre, even if it has to be the Schiffbauerdamm Theater'."

Today it is impossible to determine to what degree Tretyakov's view on art influenced Brecht; but that he certainly made a great impression is shown by the fact that Brecht repeatedly referred to Tretyakov as his "teacher". Both of them regarded art as a weapon in the political struggle. In a lecture to the Institute for the Study of Fascism in Paris on April 27th 1934, Walter Benjamin said: "Tretyakov draws a distinction between the operative and the informative writer. The mission of the operative writer is not to report, but to fight, not to be the audience but to play an active part. He defines this with details which he gives about his own activities. In 1928, in the epoch of the total collectivisation of agriculture, the slogan was 'Writers to the Collectives!', and Tretyakov went to the commune named 'Communist Lighthouse'. During two lengthy periods he spent there he undertook the following jobs: calling mass meetings; collecting money to pay the deposit on tractors; convincing individual peasants they should join the collective farms; inspecting reading rooms; establishing wall newspapers and running the collective farm paper; reporting for Moscow newspapers; bringing in radios and travelling cinemas, etc. It is by no means surprising that the book, 'Field Marshals', which Tretyakov wrote after these activities, had considerable influence on the further progress of the collective farms."

When Brecht learned in Scandinavian exile in 1938 of Tretyakov's death he wrote his poem *Are the People Infallible?*, which expressed not only sadness at Tretyakov's death, but also, astonishingly enough, his understanding of the dialectic of the difficult developments in the Soviet Union. Brecht's affirmative attitude towards the Soviet Union was never blind, his judgments were thought out and considered, he saw Soviet errors in the light of the enormous advantages and the historical progress which the Soviet Union embodied. Brecht reproved the attitude of those emigrants who had, he felt, an idealistic attitude towards the Soviet Union; they either concluded, on the basis of its errors, that it was not socialist, or they fell into the other extreme and mechanically regarded all its deeds as socialism.

"For at least a century there have been a vast quantity of

misunderstandings because many people have been unable to understand Communism as primarily a theory with regard to production," Brecht noted. "The great sentence of the Communist classics assigning to the productive forces the decisive revolutionary role against the capitalist mode of production has been little understood." Brecht found it a matter of course to apply this measure to the assessment of Soviet construction; he understood how important it was for the Soviet Union to subordinate everything to the development of productive forces. During his emigration in Scandinavia he wrote: "The immense natural difficulties of building a socialist economy at the time of a rapid and enormous worsening of the situation of the proletariat in a number of large European states produced a panic. The political conception of this panic is based upon the attitude which we find in the history of the Bolsheviks. I mean Lenin's attitude in the Brest Litovsk question, and in the question of the 'New Economic Policy'. Naturally these attitudes, however justified they were in 1918 and 1922, are *today* absolutely anachronistic, counter-revolutionary, criminal . . ."

Brecht studied the records of the first trials in the Soviet Union, which were published in German, and they occupied him to the last. However, he never forgot the context, as Gide, for instance, did. He never doubted the historical role of the Soviet Union, which had provided the basis for human freedom with the socialist mode of production; he never doubted the necessity of the proletarian revolution. In a note which he made for his "own information", as he specifically stated, Brecht wrote: "As far as the trials are concerned, it would be absolutely wrong when discussing them to adopt an attitude against the government of the Soviet Union which is organising them, since this would automatically lead in a very short time to an attitude directed against the Russian proletariat, which is today threatened with war by world fascism, and against its socialism which is in the course of construction."

In his book "der dichter und die ratio", Fritz Sternberg writes about the "unbridgeable gap" between himself and Brecht which brought their friendship to an end: "Brecht regarded the October Revolution as an extraordinarily progressive step. He transferred this attitude, without much reflection, to the Russian state of the 1930s. (...) During the period of the Hitler-Stalin Pact I did not see him, but when we met later in the war his tendency was increasingly to see only the positive elements in Russian policy and only the negative elements in the policy of the Western Powers. We had arguments, and once Brecht had a real outburst of fury."

Later, Brecht was deeply stirred by the speeches at the 20th Party Congress, but he was already in hospital and unable to make a proper analysis. But even now Brecht thought in a dialectical fashion, foreseeing that apart from its positive results, the 20th Congress would spread uncertainty, and would be exploited by the enemy. Notes which he made in summer 1956 show that his primary concern was that, in the over-zealous though certainly necessary criticism, matters of substance, the social achievements of the Soviet Union, would be called into question. He regarded the history of those years as not yet written. Brecht himself did not need to withdraw a single line. His Marxist view of the role of the individual in history had kept him from glorifying individuals.

One of Brecht's first reactions after the 20th Party Congress was to send his Lenin poems to Pasternak, asking him to translate them, as he had translated the speech delivered by Brecht in the Kremlin in May 1955 when he received the Lenin Prize. I recall his covering letter, in which he said that the right time had now come. It was at this time that Brecht met again his old friends Assia Lazis and Reich, who told him not only of the difficulties which they had lived through, but also of the fact that in these years they had never doubted Communism. They had always known that they were working for it.

Brecht visited Moscow for the first time in 1932. He went there to attend the showing of the film "Kuhle Wampe" together with his friend and collaborator Slatan Dudow who had directed the film. Brecht, together with Ottwald, had written the scenario, and Hanns Eisler had composed the music. He made his acquaintance with the country of which he had written:

In 1930 a man from Nikolayev on the Amur
Visiting Moscow, was asked how things were at home.
How should I know? he replied. The trip
Took six weeks, and in six weeks
Everything changes there.

On this first visit Brecht discovered numerous friends amongst theatre people and writers, many of whom he met again after the war. "Izvestia" reported: "Brecht's visit to our land and also his talks with our theatres about the works dedicated to the 15th anniversary of the October Revolution are steps in his development from a fellow traveller to a militant of the Communist movement."

Brecht's next visit to Moscow was in 1935. He saw the great May Day demonstration of the Moscow workers, and described its flags, emblems and slogans some years later in his poem *The Great October*. He wrote his famous poem *The Moscow Workers Take Over the Great Metro on April 27th 1935*. Olga Tretyakov relates that Brecht frequently met Tretyakov, and often saw Eisenstein. Lev Kassil guided him through the Moscow streets.

In spring 1936 Brecht travelled to Moscow to make preparations for the German-language magazine, "Das Wort", which he published together with Lion Feuchtwanger and Willi Bredel. He and Helene Weigel, who had gone with him, spoke many of the *German Satires* for the German Freedom Radio. Bernhard Reich, who met Brecht, writes: "The emigrants organised a special Brecht evening. It was held in a modest hall with room for less than one hundred." German actors in emigration sang songs from *The Three-*

penny Opera and *The Mother* for the emigrants; the audience included Béla Kun and Vilis Knorin from the Comintern, Sergei Tretyakov, and Kirsanov, who was beginning to translate Brecht's poems.

But Reich also notes that Brecht was little known in the Soviet Union at that time: "People here knew only a 'Pre-Brecht', a very talented but opinionated young man, and there were plenty of those at that time. We ourselves did not know that we were talking to a poet who deserved a place in the front rank of the greatest figures of world literature."

At that time Tretyakov had translated *The Mother, The Measures Taken* and *Saint Joan of the Stockyards* and published them with the title "Epic Theatre". The magazine "International Literature" had published a number of poems and the didactic play, *The Horatians and the Kuriatians.* Reich notes that the magazine had done this "without any particular enthusiasm," since "several leading members of the editorial board believed that Brecht's path, which deviated from the literary traditions of critical realism, had formalist features."

Of importance for Brecht was his acquaintance with Nikolai Okhlopkov; he was enthusiastic about his production of Pogodin's "Aristocrats". On Brecht's advice he staged this play for a second time in 1957. At that time (1936) Okhlopkov began to rehearse *Saint Joan of the Stockyards* in his "Realistic Theatre", but this theatre was closed during the rehearsals and the play was not produced.

In 1941 Brecht, fleeing from Finland to the United States, passed through the Soviet Union once again, via Leningrad, Moscow, Vladivostok. The question is often asked why he did not remain in the Soviet Union. The answer is as complicated as the situation was at that time. For years Brecht had refused offers to go to the United States, because in Scandinavia, near Germany, he had links with emigrant writers in many European countries. He used his U.S. visa when he had to flee from the Wehrmacht; the broad circle of former collaborators and friends already in the U.S.A. appeared to guarantee the chance for collective work once again — they included Elisabeth Hauptmann and Feucht-wanger, Eisler, Weill, Kortner, Homolka, Herzfelde, Piscator, Berthold Viertel and others.

At this time the Soviet Union had a non-aggression pact with Germany, and Brecht, who was burning to continue his battle against fascism, could not publish his attacks against fascism from the Soviet Union, with its proverbial close adherence to treaties. Brecht said later that he did not know whether he would have stayed if Hitler's attack on the Soviet Union had taken place not when he was on the ship, but a few days earlier when he was in Moscow. He pointed out, however, that the lack of work contacts would have made it difficult for him to stay in the Soviet Union. "Das Wort" had ceased publication in 1939, and the theo-retical positions adopted by the German writers in emigra-tion, under the leadership of Georg Lukács, differed from his in important points. In addition, apart from the abortive production of *The Threepenny Opera* by Tairov, practically none of Brecht's works were known. Lunacharsky, who could have helped Brecht, had died; and Tretyakov and Béla Kun, who had once supported his works, were no longer among the living. The German section of the Writers' Union gave him a friendly welcome, and Fedin and Apletin, the secretary of the Union, looked after his family and his assistants. They took Margarete Steffin who was very sick to hospital, where she had to stay, and they organised the nine-day journey to Vladivostok.

Brecht left the Soviet Union on June 13th; one day later TASS, the Soviet news agency, stated: "According to in-formation available to the U.S.S.R., Germany is adhering to the terms of the Soviet-German pact just as strictly as is the Soviet Union; in the opinion of authoritative Soviet circles rumours that Germany intends to break the pact and to attack the Soviet Union are without foundation . . ." News that Nazi Germany had attacked reached the German,

Austrian and Czechoslovak emigrants on board the "Annie Johnson" on the ninth day of their crossing.

In his great war poem written at the end of 1941 *To the German Soldiers in the East,* with its moving opening "Brothers, if I were with you," Brecht made a distinction between his unhappy, murdering and misused compatriots for whom "there is no way home," and those who drove them into battle, a clear distinction between the misled and the hangmen. He sent this poem to Moscow at the beginning of 1942 so that it might be transmitted to the German frontlines.

In all those years Brecht never wrote a line directed against the Germans as a people, just as he never wrote a line which was nationalist. The dialectic of these years, which were so bitter for Brecht, is expressed in every line of his *War primer* [a collection of photos with short comments in verse by Brecht, trans.]:

Frenzy of martial airs, storm flood of banners!
Myths of Germanic swastika crusade!
But finally there's only one thing to be done:
To find a hiding place. But you found none.

Before Moscow, man, that's where you lost your sight.
A blinded man, now you will understand.
Your mis-Leader will not take the city,
And if he took it, you could still not see it.

Look at our sons, silent and blood-spattered,
Unbound here from a frozen tank.
Even the wolf who bares his teeth
Needs refuge. Warm them, for they are cold.

Brothers, here in the distant Caucasus
I lie, a Swabian peasant, in my grave,
Shot by a Russian peasant.
I was defeated long since, in Swabia.

On that June morn near Cherbourg
A man from Maine stepped from the sea.
Reports said he came against the man from the Ruhr:
In truth it was against the man from Stalingrad.

Child on your arm, and rifle by your side,
Daring your life to bring a better life.
After this bloody struggle here's my wish for you:
To be surrounded by the children of my people.

But when we got to Moscow the red city
Men from the farms and factories confronted us.
And we were beaten in the name of all nations
Including that nation which calls itself German.

I feel as though I smashed your home
Because my brother did it, more's the shame.
Never was brighter day than when I heard
That you had beaten him and thrown him out.

In the U.S.A. Brecht worked actively in the preparations for the "Council for a Democratic Germany", formed by anti-fascists of all sections; and together with other emigrants he welcomed the foundation of the "Free Germany National Committee" in Moscow. He was one of the signatories of an appeal which stated: "We welcome the demonstration of the German prisoners-of-war and emigrants in the Soviet Union, who call upon the German people to force their oppressors to capitulate unconditionally and to fight for a real democracy in Germany."

When Brecht travelled to Moscow in 1955 for the presentation of the International Lenin Peace Prize, he had not seen the Soviet Union for fourteen years. In the meantime he had written his tragic war poems, but also *The Caucasian Chalk Circle* with its optimistic ending. He was convinced that in Germany too the valley would "belong to those who provide water so that it brings forth fruit." In the German Democratic Republic Brecht wrote his didactic poem

Training the Millet, with these cheerful lines looking towards the future:

> Dreams, golden anticipation
> See the waves of grain that's grown.
> Sower, your tomorrow's sowing
> Now, today, call it your own.

The friendly links which Brecht had in the postwar years, particularly with Soviet writers, were innumerable. So too were the visits of the theatre people, both to performances and to his house, and the encounters at peace congresses and writers' meetings — with Dymshitz, with Ehrenburg, with Fedin. And the culmination was his visit to Moscow in 1955.

In November 1954 Brecht was informed by telephone from Moscow that he had been proposed for the Lenin Prize. Two days later the decision was confirmed in a report in "Neues Deutschland". Brecht was very pleased: during these years he was scarcely ever as excited as he was that morning in the courtyard of the Berliner Ensemble when he had seen the notice in the newspaper. In a short interview which he gave to a journalist from "Izvestia" Brecht said that he was very gratified to receive the prize, and hoped that it would help him in his work for peace: "We are living in very dark times in Germany, and friendship with the Soviet Union is enormously important for us ... One of the main tasks for German writers is to work for the peaceful reunification of Germany, and the writers of the German Democratic Republic have the special task of spreading at the same time the ideas of Communism."

At this time Brecht was rehearsing Johannes R. Becher's "Winter Battle", and did not wish to interrupt his work. He named May as the time when he would visit Moscow to receive the prize. The journey was important for him, since he hoped to pick up his links with old friends, and to negotiate with publishers and theatres. At the same time he feared official ceremonies and unknown faces.

Despite this, Brecht, accompanied by Helene Weigel, started out on the journey in good spirits. In Moscow about twenty people had come to receive him — writers, theatre people, reporters, representatives of the G.D.R. embassy. Brecht and Helene Weigel received bouquets, there were shouts and laughter. Rather worried, I looked at Brecht, and could not believe my eyes: in the midst of the crowd he was walking across the airport, arm-in-arm on both sides, laughing, chatting, completely unself-conscious, completely at home.

During the ride to the Hotel Sovietskaya Brecht related what had happened. As he hesitantly went down the gangway he had suddenly spotted on the ground Comrade Apletin from the Writers' Union, smiling up at him just as he had done fifteen years earlier when Brecht had last been in Moscow in flight from the fascists in Finland. Next to him stood Okhlopkov and Fedin, whom he had also met then; and when he saw the well-known faces of friends he knew that he was in good hands. He was greatly touched by this reception.

After the presentation of the prize there was a magnificent banquet in the hotel for about one hundred guests, mainly writers and theatre people. In this cheerful company Brecht held a short speech, which I noted in shorthand on a serviette: "This was a serious day for me, and now it is ending in good cheer. This is not my first visit to your city. At the airport I was pleased to see my old friend Apletin, my mentor in 1941, as well as at earlier and later dates. My thanks to all of you, and I drink to your great new literature and to the love of this people for literature, I drink to friendship and co-operation."

Those present may have found this speech a little disjointed, and scarcely anybody could measure its importance, but it expressed Brecht's deeply felt thanks for great friendliness.

One of Brecht's visitors was Yuri Savadsky, and Brecht saw his staging of "Storm", in which he was impressed particularly by Ranyevskaya in the role of the black-market dealer. Brecht also saw Nikolai Okhlopkov's presentation of "The Young Guard", and suggested that he should re-stage "Aristocrats" which he had liked so much in 1936. Polevoy, the writer, visited him cheerfully carrying two bottles of Georgian wine, "the only proper present for a writer," as he said. Brecht also visited his old friend Kirsanov, who had translated many of his poems into Russian, and spent a happy day with Konstantin Fedin in the Writers' House in Lavrushinsky Pereulok. Brecht had invited Bernhard Reich to Moscow, and Assia Lazis came too, the old friends from Munich. Brecht negotiated with publishers and editors, and discussed with Ilya Fradkin the publication of his plays, in which he was most interested. It was very important for Brecht to see how people who had been living for a long period under socialism would react to his work. He later wrote a preface — which unfortunately arrived too late for publication — expressing his attitude:

"The playwright whose plays are presented here, lives so to speak in two eras, that of capitalism and that of socialism, during a gigantic transformation of the whole of humanity. He is seriously considering the question as to whether his works, which mostly play in capitalism, still have anything to give to the new reader. They will perhaps contribute little or nothing to the solution of the immediate and urgent everyday problems; that is what he fears. But his hope is that it may be easier to tackle the everyday problems when they are regarded in conjunction with the problems of the century. And the great problems stand in the brightest light at the time of the greatest struggles, the great revolutions. In the struggle against the old the new ideas are formulated most sharply. The great change-over which we are experiencing at present is not simply a matter of exchanging one situation for another; the new era simply is an era of change. Man will change his environment to an unprecedented degree, and at the same time change the form of social life."

When I wrote to Fradkin in January 1956 telling him that the Berliner Ensemble would abandon its plans to travel to Britain and Italy in favour of a tour to Moscow, Brecht added the words "very gladly" to my sentence. In 1955 he regretted that he had arrived in Moscow with "empty hands" as he put it. When the Berliner Ensemble made its successful tour to Moscow and Leningrad in 1957, he was no longer able to accompany it. Brecht's fear was proved baseless that his works, which played in capitalism, would not be successful in the Soviet Union.

Brecht had always regarded it as a sign of a high degree of theatre culture when one play — for example Fadeyev's "Young Guard" — was presented simultaneously at several Moscow theatres. He also admired the fact that some plays could remain on the repertoire for decades and always find an audience, and that Soviet audiences had learned the aesthetic enjoyment of the "how" of a performance. One can judge how he would have appreciated the fact that in 1964 his *Caucasian Chalk Circle* was showing simultaneously in two Moscow theatres.

By that time Brecht had proved himself a successful dramatist in the Soviet Union too. A seven-volume edition of his plays had been published as well as a volume of theoretical writings, many individual editions, and a monograph by Bernhard Reich. In the meantime Ilya Fradkin and Lev Kopelev have published monographs. More than seventy magazine articles, including important works by Singermann and Surkov, have introduced the Soviet public to Brecht's views on the theatre, and Brecht's plays have a firm place in the repertoires of the theatres. In Moscow alone there have been the programmatic presentation of *Mother Courage* by Maxim Strauch with Miss Glieser in the title role; followed by *Señora Carrar's Rifles*; *The Good Person of Sezuan*; *The Story of Simone Marchard*; *The Life of Galileo*; *The Resistible Rise of Arturo Ui*; *The Threepenny Opera*; *Man is Man; The Fear and Misery of the Third Reich; Puntila and His Servant Matti*. Plays by Brecht have been presented on the stages of the following towns: Leningrad, Riga, Lepaja, Tartu, Vilnius, Tallinn, Kemerov, Omsk, Novosibirsk, Makhachkala, Sukhumi, Vladivostok, Khabarovsk, Kharkov, Kishinev, Volgograd, Kaunas, Petrozavodsk, Otenyae, Linetsk. The most popular plays are *Puntila and His Servant Matti* and *The Threepenny Opera,* each produced ten times.

In 1955 Brecht tried to see as much of the Soviet theatre as he could; he generally changed theatres during the intermission in order to see as many actors as possible and get to know the methods of as many directors as possible. He was delighted by the production of Mayakovsky's "Bedbug" in the Satirical Theatre, directed by V. Pluchek and S. Yutkevich, with V. A. Lepko playing the part of Prisipkin. He thought that this theatre had preserved the best traditions of the Arts Theatre. In the same theatre he admired the epic manner of acting of A. V. Yatshnitzky playing Pobedonosikov in Mayakovsky's "The Bath". He was not pleased by Shakespeare's "Twelfth Night" in the branch of the Moscow Arts Theatre, mainly played by young people, which was smooth, conventional, and outdated in social concept.

He was very impressed on the other hand by the production of Ostrovsky's "Hot Heart" in the Arts Theatre, by the humour, the ideas, and the high level of the acting. He was surprised in particular that this Stanislavsky production differed from all he had read about his style of staging. He was astonished by the degree of alienation which he saw; at the same time he regretted that the class struggles in the play were not emphasised enough — for instance by Chlynov's servants criticising his attitude — so that the beauty of the play did not emerge fully. As Brecht left the theatre he sighed with amusement: "Now I shall have to defend Stanislavsky from his supporters," and added, "Now I shall have to say about him what people say about me — that the practice contradicts the theory."

The culmination of the visit was the presentation of the

Lenin Prize on the morning of May 25th 1955. Nikolai Tichonov the writer, whom Brecht had known for a long time, presented the distinction to Brecht in his capacity as chairman of the Soviet Peace Committee. "Your poems, plays and essays have become the property of the people," he said. "In the active struggle against fascism you have developed your outstanding talent. It has become a weapon in the service of peace, for the happiness of mankind."

Konstantin Fedin and Boris Polevoy congratulated Brecht in the name of Soviet authors, and Nikolai Okhlopkov and Yelena Gogoleva brought the best wishes of the theatre people. The atmosphere in the hall, which held between 300 and 400 persons, was gay and had something historic about it. Those present, mostly from the field of the arts, smiled when Nikolai Okhlopkov went to the speaker's desk and addressed Brecht — for everybody knew that 20 years earlier his theatre had been closed during his Brecht production. It was more than just the presentation of a prize.

And then Brecht read his speech, with a firm voice, very quiet and very serious. He looked back on his development and what he had learned: "The most important lesson was that a future for humanity can only be seen 'from below', from the point of view of the oppressed and exploited. Only he who fights with them fights for humanity."

Brecht said later that he had been grateful for the extreme simplicity of the ceremony, without show, with no display. Immediately after the ceremony he was surrounded by reporters and photographers: he became noisy and jolly, and next day his speech was reported in all the papers, including those reaching Moscow from the G.D.R. Today sentences from the speech are used as slogans, for instance the fine sentence from the introduction:

"Whatever they are told, the peoples know: Peace is the Alpha and Omega of all human activities, all production, and all arts, including the art of living."

Ernst Schumacher
He Will Remain
1956

I first became acquainted with Brecht in 1944, when the swarms of bombers which preceded the prodigal son were getting as far as Munich. In the summer term of that year, Professor Arthur Kutscher was lecturing to the students of the Ludwig-Maximilian University on "Post-Impressionist Drama". Kutscher seldom had so many hearers as he had for these lectures. Dead expressionism, the vanished 1920s — and that was what Kutscher had to lecture about if he was to keep to his subject — exerted their magic on a new generation, partly just because these themes had been banished by the Nazis.

I still do not know why Kutscher was lecturing on this touchy subject. It may have been because in the previous term he had lectured on "The Drama of Naturalism and Impressionism", and like a real pedant he simply went on where he had left off. Perhaps it was opposition to the Nazis, who cannot have welcomed the fact that the students now heard the names of the burned and the banned, even if Kutscher clung to the official evaluations. Possibly he did it for opportunistic motives, thinking of the times to come, after the war which was already lost, when he would be able to say: I did not neglect the real Germany. Or perhaps it was simply a remnant of his old love for that period, for those writers with whom, it was well known, he had been linked in many ways.

But whatever the reason Professor Kutscher, a massive figure, already bowed with age, leaned on his desk and with a warped voice, sometimes very loud because of his deafness, talked about Wilhelm von Scholz, Erwin Guido Kolbenheyer, Hanns Johst, about the "folkish" and the "national" writers down to the very last Baumann. Had students fought for places in the too small lecture theatre to listen to this? But Kutscher did not disappoint them. After Herbert Eulenberg, Karl Schönherr, Hermann Bahr, Anton Wildgans he proceeded to Klabund, Franz Werfel, Ernst Barlach, August Stramm, Paul Kornfeld, Walter Hasenclever, Ernst Toller, to the expressionists and the generation of dramatists who followed, whose works had been consigned to the flames in 1933, who had been banished from the libraries, who had themselves been driven out or killed by the Nazis. Kutscher had no hesitation in describing them in the words prescribed by the murderers; his evaluations were often inept and sordid. Referring to Eulenberg he said: "He has no feeling of responsibility." For him, Ernst Barlach was "the product of a chaotic period and of the critics of his era." August Stramm was a "triumph of the un-intellectual." He claimed that Ferdinand Bruckner had aimed at achieving "the cheapest effects on the mob."

Despite all this, every lecture had an almost magical effect; this came about when Kutscher picked up one of the books lying next to his desk, and read from the works of the writer he had just mauled. It happened time and again that some of his listeners laughed or showed indignation. Despite this, the "banned and burned literature" had a strong effect upon the young people.

In one of these lectures I first learned about Brecht's plays. Kutscher did not neglect to introduce Brecht as a half-Jew; but then he gave a full survey of his early works and his theatre theories. In my notes I wrote about *Drums in the Night*: "Prisoner-of-war finds his girl in the arms of a war profiteer. Becomes Spartakist." Talking about *Man is Man* Kutscher said: "Like a Cheap Jack, Brecht repeatedly addresses explanations to his audience."

He forgave his former pupil *The Threepenny Opera* but he did not forgive him *Saint Joan of the Stockyards*. Speaking of this play, he said: "Here the dissolution of the drama is complete. Things go so far that four pigs appear and sing. Red-hot fanaticism, the coldest cynicism, a combination of Christians and oxen. Bolshevik blasphemy. Hostility towards western culture." And this was followed by a condemnation of Brecht which has made me laugh ever since, although it is not original, but simply an adaptation of Wieland's verdict upon Heinse: "Bert Brecht is the apocalyptic beast in German literature."

As chance would have it, that summer I inherited from an uncle a complete set of the Catholic magazine "Hochland". Looking through the literary section, I discovered in the February 1932 issue an essay by Karl Thieme entitled: "The Devil's Prayerbook?" In this article I read that Christian fundamental truths had never been presented "more simply, directly and unambiguously" than by the atheist Brecht. I read the apparently peculiar anecdote which related that when Brecht had been asked by the magazine "Dame" which book meant the most to him, he had replied: "You will laugh: the Bible." I read further: "We know nobody who has cast in the classical mould, as he has done in his *Measures Taken*, Bolshevism at its coldest, at its most hostile to eternity." But despite this, no, just because of this, Brecht was, the article stated, the only one worth arguing with.

But neither Kutscher's condemnation nor Thieme's "elevation" could impress me half as much as the extracts from Brecht's works. The spirit of the century, of the new age, spoke to me from these passages. I started to search for Brecht's works, to search for the era to be won.

Kutscher regarded me with a superior air, with astonishment, and with misapprobation, when I asked him to lend me Brecht's works. He could not take such a responsibility, he told me in a grudging tone. In the university library and the state library Brecht was in the "poison cabinet", and the library of the German studies department did not have his books.

The war came to an end. *Freedom and Democracy* entered

my homeland [*Freedom and Democracy* is the title of one of Brecht's works, trans.]. Newspapers and magazines sometimes printed poems or scenes by Brecht. I learned that Brecht was living in America. Searching for people who knew him, I located Jacob Geis, a friend from his youth. One Sunday I went out to visit him on the Ammersee. Leaving him my identity card as security, I was allowed to borrow the first volume of the collected *Experiments*. Geis was also kind enough to lend me the *Household Homilies*. He told me stories about Brecht, reported with obvious pride that he and Brecht together had concocted the songs for *Mahagonny* in a cowshed on the Ammersee, and that he had been the first person to produce *Man is Man*, in Darmstadt. On a monstrous old book-keeping typewriter I typed out, page by page, the *Experiments*, since Brecht's works had still not been made available to the public in the state library and the university library. I decided to write my doctorate on Brecht's early plays, and got in touch with Kutscher. It was a rainy day when I visited him in his make-shift quarters in Schwabing. He held his hand behind his ear as I explained my plan to him, then shook his head. No, he couldn't do it, he said. He admitted quite frankly that he had objections to taking up cudgels with the faculty in support of a thesis about Brecht the arch-Bolshevik, since he himself had not yet passed through the process of denazification. "The subject is too political," he told me repeatedly, stressing again and again his precarious situation. I did not abandon my plan. Since I had not even got my hands on all the works which Brecht had written before he emigrated, I applied direct to Brecht, after discovering his address in Santa Monica. I never received a reply.

Later when I first met Brecht in Berlin, I told him all this. He laughed. But it was not a hearty laugh, and not a mocking laugh; it was a depressed and knowing laugh. "Yes, yes," he said, "yes, yes, that's the way it is." He walked up and down deep in thought, sucking on his cigar. Perhaps it was because of this that he later answered all my questions with exemplary patience and forbearance; questions which were not to be found in the questionaires so popular in those days, questions which every now and then led him to sigh regretfully and slightly ironically and say: "Yes, if I only remembered."

In later encounters I realised that Brecht regarded German literary scholars, including the Marxists, with a certain sorrowing sympathy, because they are "so awfully clever, and so seldom lay an egg." But that evening, in his house in Weissensee, he seemed to be impressed by the tragicomical search for Brecht staged by this unknown student from his own corner of Germany. Probably he regarded his patience and his answers as a contribution to that process of "ideology smashing" which he described as the most important task of the theatre and the playwright in a discussion with students in Leipzig in February 1948.

On the pages which follow I do not intend to speak of his decency, of his lasting readiness to supply me with information, his hospitality, his concern about personal affairs. Others who lived together with him, who had closer contacts, who worked with him every day, can report more suitably on his basic friendliness. I should prefer to emphasise some of his views on art and literature in our age, views which he expressed in conversations and which appear to me to be characteristic of him and important for us.

In September last year Brecht took a look at the production of *The Good Person of Sezuan* in Frankfurt and then came on to Munich to discuss with Hans Schweikart the presentation of this play at the Kammerspiele Theatre. He sent me a message that he would have a few hours to spare on the afternoon before he left; if I had time and interest I should visit him in his hotel. Our conversation immediately turned to Brecht's next plans. He told me that he wanted to prepare a production of *The Life of Galileo* with Ernst Busch in the title role.

A short while earlier I had read the book "The Drama of Albert Einstein" by Antonia Vallentin. In my opinion the authoress should have spoken not simply of the drama of his life, but also of the tragedy. This tragedy consisted of the fact that Einstein's formula of the "harmony of the worlds" had been one of the keys to the destruction of the world; that the pioneer of the anti-war movement and international conscientious objection had become the advocate of the atomic bomb; that he had to watch while this frightful weapon, against his urging, was dropped without warning on an open city; that Einstein had fled from militarist Germany only, as he himself said, to find Potsdam in the United States. I said that I thought that this life was just as important a study for a dramatist as the life of Galileo, and, I continued, it would only be logical if Brecht concerned himself with it.

Brecht listened attentively, walking up and down the room and smoking his cigar; as always when listening he intermittently jerked up his head and held it aslant. I knew that he had long been moved by the phenomenon of Einstein, and that he was very interested in theoretical physics. At that meeting he left the question open as to whether he had already, without saying anything, started to work on the material. (Shortly afterwards he asked me to obtain for him Leopold Infeld's report on his work with Einstein, which had appeared in instalments in the "Deutsche Woche"; and a little later still there was a note in the press that Brecht was working on an Einstein play.) Brecht pointed out that it was very difficult to deal with contemporary problems in a play. He preferred to locate the problems of the present in the past, as Shakespeare had done. The reason was simple: the problems could be shown from a distance. They were thus more easy to understand, and could be presented in an unusual form which awakened the interest.

I countered that *The Fear and Misery of the Third Reich* and *Señora Carrar's Rifles* were convincing witnesses against his theory. He immediately retorted: "But the effect is far less than that of the plays written in the other form, for instance *The Chalk Circle*." He continued: "The real influencing must be done at a greater depth, less limited by time. The problems of today," he went on, bringing his idea to a point, "can only be grasped by the theatre in so far as they are problems of comedy. All other problems exclude themselves from direct presentation. Comedy allows of solutions; tragedy, if you still believe in its potentiality, does not." He recalled his *Puntila*. Comedy allowed, even forced, a distancing and thus made possible an inspection of the relations. Irony made it possible to bare a problem, and thus to penetrate and deal with it. He continued: "How would you show the life of Rosa Luxemburg, her tragic struggle and end? I have tried, but I never got further than the prologue. I have discussed it with other people, and we reached agreement that a truthful study would only deepen the conflict in the working-class movement, would only re-open old wounds. Face to face with the reactionaries, because of the necessity of consolidating our own ranks, this would have been irresponsible. The struggle between Rosa and Lenin about the better type of party, about the spontaneity theory, was not yet forgotten. In a sort of way I would have to have argued against the Party. But I have no intention of chopping off my foot just to prove that I am handy with an axe."

I insisted that such tactical considerations did not prove that contemporary themes could not be shown except in comedy form. I recalled *The Mother*. Brecht replied that *The Mother* was already historically alienated. He responded to my objection: "All right, let's assume that you have a great contemporary subject, and there is no worry about the effect, no scruple about the Party line. But a great contemporary subject will necessarily include the working-class element, either actively or passively. And there you immediately have an enormous difficulty. The workers, in contrast to the bourgeoisie, have never taken the stage as a type, but as a mass, and they will always remain a mass. I emphasise remain, since this is their main strength. But for the theatre you need types; quantity, that very particular form of quality, can only be shown with the greatest difficulty, although it is just this which is typical for our society."

Brecht then approached the problem from the other side: "There are Marxist experts in aesthetics who claim that the novel is the most suitable art form for dealing with the phenomena of our day. The novel allows us to depict both the individual and the mass. But in this case why are our novels so inadequate compared to those of the bourgeoisie? I do not think it is because our novelists cannot invent plots which make sense. The reason is that the proletarian hero is far more strongly collective, far more strongly mass, than the bourgeois hero could ever be. And the actions of this mass, even in the novel, can only be described, not "fashioned" as some people say. For this reason we have in our novels lots of super-heroes, and no heroes who impress us. The positive type of this century can no longer be shown in the old form, from the old standpoint. The new forms still have to be developed. Whether such new forms will be available without introducing 'alien elements', for instance introducing film into theatre, remains to be seen."

A conversation in the past winter confirmed how Brecht was grappling with this question. Brecht said: "In your book on my dramatic experiments before 1933 you stated that the heroine of *Saint Joan of the Stockyards* had a counterpart of the same rank in the capitalist Mauler, but not amongst the workers who appear in the play. Those, you say, appear only as a mass, act only as a chorus, have no face. I have thought about this. But how could it be changed? If I convert the anonymous workers' leader into Joe the trade union official, or Bill the Communist, when I give him a recognisable face, then my play about the social reformer, the petty-bourgeois girl, will become quite a different play. And how can masses be shown except as a chorus? Of course it cannot remain as it is if we want to stage the play. The representatives of the working class must at least have a face, that is clear. I shall have to give more thought to this."

In our conversation in Munich which I have already men-

tioned, Brecht said that he was naturally completely in favour of treating contemporary themes in a contemporary
form; it was vitally necessary for the theatre to experiment
in this direction. But he appeared to give such experiments
only the chance of being "test art", in the way in which in-
dustry arranges destructive tests of products in order to confirm theoretical analyses.

Once he had begun to organise this idea in theses, it gave
him pleasure to overstate it. He began to urge the use of the
parable-play as the best of all forms: "If you want to smash
false convictions and shape correct convictions, then you
must reveal the man to the man, you might say restore him
to consciousness. You cannot do this by confronting him with
people like himself. Josef knows Josef so well that Josefs
mean nothing to him. You can't talk with the owner of a
house which is in flames, but you can talk with the commander of the fire brigade. In one word, the business has to
be alienated. The more simply the better. For this reason the
parable form is still the best. Do you think that Lenin spoke
by chance about climbing high mountains? This made the
difficulties which at that time confronted a part of the socialist movement so clear to everybody that at the same time
they lapped up the theoretical considerations.

"Let us assume," Brecht continued his deductions, "that
The Good Person of Sezuan was not written in parable
form. I would then have to show a proletarian who became
a member of the bourgeoisie or of the petty bourgeoisie, and
subsequently, of course, has to change his tune completely
in order to remain bourgeois or petty bourgeois; that is to
say a negative hero. The bourgeois would say: Look, we
are not so wicked after all, and would introduce quite different problems with which I want nothing to do, for instance in the sense of the 'bourgeois as a nobleman'. (In his
'Bed-bug' Mayakovsky showed the proletarian as a bourgeois.) The result would be a comedy in the style of *Puntila*
roughly on the theme 'riches impose obligations'. In order
to bar this road to the heroes and traders, all that remains

is the parable form, which discloses without trouble and without possibility of evasion how shabby and imperfect a society is in which a man can only be good and decent when he is regularly bad. Without it being stated, everybody is forced to the conclusion that this society deserves to be changed, indeed that it must be changed. In the field of 'direct realism' this could only have been done with difficulty. Such a play would be ponderous compared to a parable-play; it would not be very jolly or amusing. I am firmly convinced that with the increase in civilisation in Communism the parable has a great future, since it enables the truth to be presented so elegantly."

I objected that the parable form also carries with it the danger of being undialectic. It is too general and in a particular historical situation can be as misleading as some proverbs. I reminded him of *The Round-Heads and the Pointed-Heads.* The parable presents the social developments in Nazi Germany in such a way that at the conclusion the Nazis reach an agreement with the rich Jews at the cost of the poor Jews and the poor Aryans. In reality, however, racialism had been far more brutal: the rich Jews too had been victims. Brecht defended himself, stating that in a certain way he had been in the right. The outcome of the war and the following period had proved that "Aryan" finance capital in Germany, which had supported Hitler, had made common cause during and after the war with "Jewish-related" finance capital in the United States, at the cost of the exploited in both countries. He would not, however, deny that this parable did not quite click. However, the parable offered the advantage of simplicity and easy assimilation, the opportunity of publishing truth in an indirect fashion, something still of great importance in our century. In addition it made it possible to mobilise forces with the use of pathos; pathos was always questionable because it was superficial. "The parable is much more cunning than any other form. Lenin used parables not as an idealist but as a materialist. A parable made it possible for him to untangle a complicated subject. For the playwright the parable is the egg of Columbus, since it is concrete in abstraction, making essentials clearly visible."

Brecht continued: "I gave you my *Turandot* adaptation, the *Congress of Whitewashers*. You will recall how the intellectuals are asked why rice has become so expensive, and why there is such disorder in the state. One of the intellectuals comes fairly near to the truth, but simultaneously the bread-basket hanging before his nose rises ever higher in the air. This is so visible that everybody understands the conflicts which confront intellectuals in certain situations when they carry their thoughts on their tongues."

Visibility and understandability meant for Brecht enjoyment. In a talk in Buckow — after I had read *Turandot* — Brecht complained about the obvious decline in the ability to enjoy. "Why is something 'art'?" he enquired. "Obviously because it gives enjoyment. But we no longer have proper healthy appetites; nothing tastes good any more. Instead of taste we have curious overbred tongues with miserable taste buds. Our glands no longer function, our mouths no longer water at the sight of meat."

He wanted to prepare and serve his meals in such a manner that they would revive the stunted sense of taste. He wanted to make a theatre that it would be a pleasure to watch. Such a theatre could only be one of "well-tempered sensuousness", of compressed realism. Speaking of superficial realism he said: "You get too much served up, they expect you to overeat yourself on reality. Too much luxuriance, always with your nose in the meat, you don't get a chance to taste anything. Everything is so genuine that it's spooky. I'm absolutely in favour of luxury, but it is still something rare, something you must know how to appreciate; and this demands the exertion of learning. When luxury is no longer rare, then the liberty to refrain from luxury must be maintained. You must enjoy consciously and be able to enjoy."

He hated nothing more than the temptation to unconsciousness, to "let yourself be engulfed". Tempting people to do this he abhorred more than this yielding weakness itself. The "sleep-lullers" was what he once called those play-smiths who base their plays on "entering into feelings". "Science consists of confrontation. A zoologist does not enter into a locust; at the most he presents it. We, the theatre people, cannot simply go on behaving as though we were living in the pre-scientific age. Apart from that, it is impudent and at the same time dangerous and irresponsible to demand that the spectator should leave his brain in the cloakroom."

Brecht's epic theatre was designed as the theatre of the scientific age, a theatre that conveyed insight and knowledge in a sensual way, and in which understanding and enjoyment were one and the same for the audience. He repeatedly emphasised that the idea was derived from many sources: the acting of Herr Steinrück, the actor, which had been completely without any "coziness"; the "political theatre" of Erwin Piscator; American behaviourism, which had drawn his attention to the study of human behaviour; the writings of scientific socialism, which had made this behaviour understandable to him as class-dependent; the gestures of Charlie Chaplin; eastern Asian theatre, which had shown him the importance of distance and dignified simplicity; the agit-prop theatre of the Communist Party which had helped him to grasp the means and methods which can make the theatre an instrument for changing the world; Bavarian and Scandinavian folk theatre, which contributed sensuality; constant practical co-operation with actors like Helene Weigel, Ernst Busch, Charles Laughton, which converted the theory into practice; and, odd though it sounds, the reading of detective stories which gave him relaxation, but also exercised his intellect.

He never missed a chance to point out the enormous difficulties which had confronted and still confronted epic theatre. Last summer, speaking of the misunderstandings which arise solely from the term "epic theatre", he said:

"I must admit that I have not been able to make it clear that the 'epic' element in my theatre applies to the social category, not the aesthetic-formal category. I am at present working on an amplification of my *Small Organon*, and I am asking myself seriously whether it would not be more practical to drop entirely the term epic theatre." He continued ironically: "Epic theatre rather resembles the Catholic Church; by the time the Catholic Church had dealt with the heresies it was ripe for retirement, since a new age had dawned." I replied: "The difference is that the Catholic Church became superfluous, but the main elements of your theatre will be obvious and indispensable for the new age." Brecht commented: "In a certain way you may be right, since, for example it is as yet quite impossible to perform epically. The actors would have to be Marxists and the audience as well. And where on earth do you get them? Some people cannot get along without projecting themselves, and the other part cannot do without suggestion. The lantern of illusion, the great moon of deception must shine. I am not opposed to the light which must always shine on all reality in the theatre. But neither actors nor public should forget that the spells must serve to reveal the real world, and the magical light must x-ray it. Oh, the epic theatre . . ."

For a moment Brecht appeared to abandon himself to fantasy. He had before his eyes a world which would regard his theatre as just as normal as the bourgeois world regards its theatre. But he immediately restrained his galloping thoughts. Apparently abruptly he continued: "And from the alienation effect, generally only the effect remains, separated from its social points of reference, separated from its purposes." I countered that even then it fulfilled the function of making "sleep-lulling" more difficult. Brecht commented: "You know, human nature knows how to adapt itself just as well as the rest of organic matter. Man is even capable of regarding atomic war as something normal, so why should he not be capable of dealing with an affair as small as the alienation effect so that he does not need to open his eyes. I can imagine that one day they will only be able to feel their old pleasure when the alienation effect is offered. But it is a good thing that the new consciousness, on which I am counting with my theatre, will be enforced by external circumstances."

I replied: "You attach too little importance to your contribution to this changing of consciousness." As in other conversations he was stimulated to answer the contradiction with one of his own, convinced that even exaggeration would produce a more useful result than agreement. At another time he would have replied with an ironical attack upon the "unique value of art", consisting in the fact that it, like everything else, is transitory. But at this hour he denied himself such a polemic. Rather reflectively he replied: "Georg Kaiser succeeded Gerhart Hauptmann on the throne of German drama. Since Kaiser died, I am there, whether people like it or not. But will my consequences be greater than theirs? Will I last longer as a living effective force?

"The answer is naturally yes," he said, becoming ironical, "even if only because I wrote the sentence 'First a full belly, and then come morals.' Something like that lasts."

I am, however, convinced that the consequences of Brecht, his "staying with us", will be lasting: and not just because of this sentence.

Werner Mittenzwei
Brecht 1973 – Speech
on his 75th Birthday

Brecht was not particularly fond of commemorating specific calendar dates. In his opinion it was difficult enough to pick the real turning-points. A body of work like that of Brecht, which is so multifold, so penetrating in social and artistic development, naturally has its own turning-points, its own caesura in effect. There is, however, always cause to question the work of a writer, and to give an answer as to how it has been utilised by us, how it has been further developed.

I.

Reflecting upon the transitory nature of works and ideas, the young Brecht wrote: "I have no demand that my thoughts should remain; but I would like them all to be consumed, transposed, used." It was never irrelevant to him whether a thought was lasting; but he understood "lasting" in the sense of "productive". The thought should enter into undertakings of a different nature, should continue to be operative in future exertions. Thus an appreciation of Brecht can only consist of investigating in how far, and in what way, his work has remained productive for the solution of our problems. This demands that we should at the same time examine ourselves to see what demands we have made upon the writer, what we have mastered, and where solutions have been absent.

In the past few years Brecht has not been so hotly discussed as in previous years. In the international discussion his crudest slanderers have lost their credit as a result of his world fame and the lasting magnetic power of his works.

Brecht's position in world literature, his contribution to the progress of socialist art, is today generally accepted. A number of important writers and artists in the German Democratic Republic acknowledge Brecht as their teacher, the one from whom they first learned how art can be made in the sense of "increasingly strong, tender and daring humanity." There is nothing surprising about the multiplicity of references to Brecht and connections with Brecht. He made many things really known for the first time, or taught us how to see them. He demonstrated how old beauties and new beauties should be seen; he gave hints and tips, and above all he taught the dialectical use of methods. At an earlier period the fear was often voiced that his great prototype could lead to simple imitation, but this fear has proved to be unfounded. His pupils, who grasped the dialectic of his methods, schooled themselves in the artistic sovereignty of leaving behind them that already tried, and went new ways.

In our Republic, Brecht's books are in the hands that he wished. They are read today with less exertion than in former years, but still with increasing pleasure and enjoyment. Brecht's plays have a firm place in the repertoire of our theatres. The literature about Brecht grows from year to year to a degree scarcely to be surveyed. In the international field there is a real inflation of titles like "Brecht and ..." He is compared to the most various figures of world literature and contemporary literature. Even non-Marxist students of literature and the theatre are now trying to do more justice to Brecht's socio-political stand. As a result, new and stimulating studies have been made; but new legends are also being created. Brecht himself gave much consideration to the way in which the heritage of world literature could be made accessible in its original boldness and freshness; now he and his work form part of the heritage which the working class does not simply cultivate, but with which it "works" as Lenin said. With his works the working class grasps the meaning of past fights and exertions, enjoys life, and seeks to overcome present difficulties.

Despite all this we should be dissatisfied rather than satisfied. The positive sides of this "situation report" are incontestable; but it cannot be overlooked that the present development of literature in our country takes the view that Brecht lies behind it rather than before it. The regard for his multifarious work and his theoretical arsenal has not diminished; but it is felt that enough of this storehouse of treasure has been assimilated. Now new considerations are needed for new problems. For this reason the question is being posed increasingly plainly: How do we get further? How do we proceed "beyond Brecht"? Such a tendency lies fully in Brecht's spirit; he wished that his thoughts should be consumed, transposed, used. There is nothing disquieting in this tendency; this is the unrest needed by every art searching for new paths. What would be disquieting would be a simple "doing it differently" without a real analysis of the new social developments which demand different methodological solutions; for them there would be the danger that valuable socialist cultural lessons of the past half century would be lost.

This attitude in our present literary situation, of getting beyond Brecht, should not be confused with the erroneous attempts to overcome Brecht without ever having understood him, nor with the tendency to "harmlessise" Brecht's society-changing art.

In the course of the 1968 Brecht Dialogue in this very hall, Max Frisch pronounced his hotly debated sentence about the "decisive ineffectiveness" of Brecht the classic writer, a sentence which proved greatly premature. Today, in a variety of places, it can be seen more clearly how Brecht envisaged his idea of an intervening, society-changing theatre. The charge made against such a theatre that it is utopian comes from those only prepared to regard theatre qua theatre, and not to grasp it in its social function, as a link in the social entirety. Some bourgeois critics charge that

Brecht has become something for gourmets, and say that the audiences of today relish the *Song of the Class Enemy* just as they do an aria by Puccini; we could ask which audiences these critics are speaking of. But I regard such a statement as completely untrue. The essential factor is which social forces take possession of Brecht's works, and in what way. What has really changed, particularly in an audience in the developed socialist society, is the distance between the fighting value and the artistic value. The audience no longer views this as an antinomy. Pleasures do not obstruct the struggle, they do not use up revolutionary impulses; on the contrary they encourage and give wings to the readiness to change those things which hamper human productivity. In his last years Brecht drew repeated attention to the fact that it is in works of art that mankind becomes aware of the defeats and the victories in the great social struggle. In art we can enjoy the vindication of great militant standpoints. The pleasure strengthens vitality and readiness for struggle. Brecht regarded as completely undialectical the opinion that all art consumes itself affirmatively. Since this opinion does not reflect real historic experience and popular wisdom, he regarded it as much too narrow, too weak, and in the final analysis useless in the programme of struggle of the revolutionary working class.

In recent years in particular the great measure could be noted in which his works had become an expression and a part of the international class struggle. Everywhere in the world where people are struggling for their liberation, to improve their lives, his writings bring aid and impulse. The conditions of struggle in the anti-imperialist liberation fight vary greatly in individual countries, but Brecht may always be found in the armoury. One of the main reasons for the international function and effectiveness of this writer is the close connection between Brecht and the revolutionary party of the working class. His work not only reflects the world-revolutionary process following the October Revolution, it is also a direct part of this liberation struggle.

When we speak of the internationalist attitude of his writing we must also note the deep and lasting impression that Lenin made upon Brecht. It was Hanns Eisler who emphasised that Brecht had learned more from Lenin than is generally known, and that none of his biographies have shown properly this enormous influence. Eisler declared that Brecht must be regarded as a pupil of Lenin. In order to varnish over this influence, bourgeois literary experts are at present busy weaving a number of legends. They are searching for new prototypes and teachers for Brecht, in order to foist upon him a special "individual Marxism". With such attempts in view, Eisler, referring to Lenin's influence on Brecht's work, stated: "When we speak about Brecht we are in a position of struggle, particularly in the capitalist countries. We are fighting for Brecht. They have got to swallow Brecht, and we shall only allow them to swallow Brecht thorns and all."

Brecht learned from Lenin that neither reformist half-measures nor leftist utopias could help the working class to victory. For Brecht the truth was always concrete, in Lenin's sense. The criterion for him was the real socialism as constructed by the workers after the October Revolution. This was the reason for his sharp polemics in his American exile against theoreticians like Adorno, Horkheimer and Marcuse. Brecht was repeatedly moved to polemics against the "Frankfurtists", as he called them, because of their superficial treatment of certain basic principles of Marxism, their complete lack of interest in real social changes, and their obvious lack of materialist perception. Brecht only developed a really effective revolutionary mode of thought in alliance with the working class and the collective of its Marxist party. Brecht, who is regarded as one of the most original thinkers of our century, had no time for an attitude based upon recognising only one's own conscience, trusting only to one's own thoughts, creeping back after each failed experiment to one's own cave. Brecht put it like this: "To depend only upon your own strength means usually to depend also and mainly upon the suddenly emergent strength of strangers."

When the broadest possible solution is sought for the most urgent difficulties, Brecht's works are consulted. The many-sidedness of these works has become vividly apparent to us through their differing application in various countries. Occupied as we have been with the problems of staging and the historical-philosophical content of the great Brecht plays, many of us have scarcely noted the art-theoretical and culture-theoretical consequences of the renaissance of Brecht's didactic plays, and in particular his theories of didactic theatre, in the ranks of the anti-imperialist liberation movement.

The real discovery for me at the 1968 Brecht Dialogue was that it was impossible to bring about a narrowing-down to one problem or a few questions which everybody was interested in discussing. In the various countries quite different portions of his works and his thoughts had their appeal at that date, and this is even more so today. According to the traditions of the individual countries and the situation in their political struggle, varying parts of his works stand at the centre of interest. Just because Brecht's work is not simply an object of the international art market, but a factor in the present world-revolutionary process, his work is utilised in a manner dependent upon the prevailing political circumstances. The result is that in one country the didactic plays and the theory of didactic theatre are of greater interest than the great plays; and that in another country certain parts of his theatrical theory and theatrical method are of greater interest than the plays themselves. In a third country, finally, Brecht the Marxist philosopher and social scientist may for a period stand more in the foreground than Brecht the writer. For this reason we should, in judging his effect, devote more attention to Brecht in the round. During the 1960s attention tended to be concentrated on Brecht the dramatist due to the magnificent productions and the discovery of the poetry and the theatrical richness of Brecht's plays.

We should of course realise that no playwright, however great, can continue uninterruptedly to exert, with constant intensity, influence on artistic progress and the growing generation. There are intensive phases, in which the strong stimuli often lead as far as imitation; and then there are the enduring, lasting effects of poetic work on contemporary output. Effects of this sort are often not to be noted at first sight; they can only be ascertained in the analysis of a longer period. It is precisely these phases, during which it appears that the intensive influence of a great work is declining because of changing conditions, which demand thorough analysis and collective discussion. It is in blind alleys of this sort that the new solutions are produced.

2.

The urgent questions of aesthetics, which many writers and artists believe demand new methodological consideration in our socialist artistic development, include the question of the presentation of the individual, individuality. Tracking down and blocking in the individuality of figures located in new social relations have become a field of experimentation for many writers and artists. In the search for such considerations and methodological solutions they often believe that they are not served well enough by Brecht, since in his time he was confronted with other questions. From Brecht they have learned how social events can be depicted in a great and exemplary form. Now, however, the main thing is to give stronger expression to the individuality of a figure, without forgetting that every figure lives amidst a society which influences him to a greater or lesser degree. In this way contemporary socialist art practice, within the framework of the dialectic, guides interest away from the individual and the social, and more towards the other side of the dialectical process: the presentation of individuality.

This interest in the individual, in individuality, should not be misunderstood as a retreat from socially oriented art which regards its main task as throwing light on social relationships. Cultural development does not proceed so mechanically that previous efforts to master the objective considerations now become converted into a longing for more subjectivity. Theoretically the problems are in the main solved, it is believed. The individual is regarded as a social being, only capable of developing his faculties in all directions in community with others. However, the prerequisites are the economic-social conditions which make possible, as Marx defined it, the development-jump from a "seeming society" to a "genuine society".

When Brecht began to develop his ideas about a new literature in the 1920s, the problem of individuality was posed from a different angle. In his writings Brecht describes how he was often surprised by the way in which his fellow writers were repeatedly capable of discovering in individuality a new nuance, an emotion never before described, an unknown peculiarity. This was the description of individual "variety" in the "seeming society". The increasing human alienation in capitalism, and the connected hypostatisation rather than the release of his real potentialities, produced a variety of external attributes. In this manner the decay rather than the richness of the individual was given expression. Brecht was perfectly right when he saw that this was not producing individuals. Instead bourgeois "profiles" were being produced, in fact the whole of art was being reduced to the level of "profile portraits". In the 1920s, when Brecht took a position of opposition to individual-centricity in literature, he coined the decisive phrase: "The individual falls as the focus." This was a challenge, and a radical breach with all earlier aesthetics. After this, Brecht began to develop his ideas about the dialectic of individual and mass as a decisive aesthetic question. He declared that hitherto the problem of the mass had always been produced by the individual. It was precisely this mode of observation which appeared to him to be the great obstacle to the ability to demonstrate on the stage the typical course of a human life.

This "observation of the individual" was developed by Brecht in opposition to the individualist bourgeois attitude to literature. But this situation of conflict did not make Brecht the dialectician one-sided, with the result that for our times, in which we certainly do not regard everything from the individual, his theory and practice of art have important implications. In the years of his exile and of socialist construction in the G.D.R. he always emphasised that when describing the objective social facts one should never forget that the individual is a fact too. Just because the individual is an inseparable part of the social process, any confrontation between the individual and society is undialectical and does not lead to a solution in the aesthetic sense. Brecht's concentration on social events as mass events does not exclude the "great individual" but makes it understandable for the audience by explaining it on the basis of class movements. At the same time Brecht explained that the abstract "social character" of a figure in its artistic fashioning was only an "imaginary line". The writer is always most successful when he does not completely determine the movements of the individual, when he leaves his characters some elbowroom. For Brecht the individuality of a figure was a matter of major importance, and this is shown by his plays. He regarded the approach to a properly understood individuality as blocked, however, if every society was regarded simply as an assemblage of individuals. Such a method of viewing would reverse the basic situation; as Brecht said, the mass events would be regarded from the individual. The artist cannot approach the task of describing the individual by psychologising society. In order to express artistically the contradictory nature and the uniqueness of the individual, Brecht complied with the sentence written by Marx: "Society does not consist of individuals, but expresses the sum of the connections and relations in which these individuals stand to one another."

Brecht's understanding in this field caused him to organise his artistic practice in the direction of his observation of human conduct. Man was not sufficiently informative for him either as an individual or as a social character, a type. How people behave to each other under different circumstances appeared to him to be much more interesting; how they speak about politics, how they handle their tools, how they react to new ideas, how they assess actions, how they master life. In this manner Brecht developed a high degree of realism in details, producing a contradictory many-layered individuality, making it clear that history, as Marx said, produced the individual. He liked to have this sort of individuality imparted even to the gestures and the rhythm of speech of his characters. He was not satisfied with "characteristics" as the random psychological decoration of a figure. He demanded the artistic creation of complicated reactions and movements of the individual produced by the movements of social forces, and this in the smallest detail, gesture, nuance. No amount of work, no amount of observation was too much for him in catching the individual in the multiplicity of his relationships. This is also the methodological pivot which is also so important for artistic production today. It is not some sort of individualism which leads to the presentation of great and contradictory figures of rich individuality, but the exact observation and artistic adaptation of those changes which may be detected in the lives and the relationships of man. This is where the study of Brechtian methods should be pursued in order to open up new roads in the arts. It was Brecht who showed us that socialist art can use old material, but that it must obtain its poetry from the new reality.

Brecht himself attempted to master from many sides the dialectic of the individual and the social aspects. In his collected works we note two different solutions. One method leads to those figure-types best matured in Galileo and Puntila. The other method leads to the didactic play, to the *Fatzer* fragment. Brecht wanted his plays to be judged according to the most varying potentialities. In a diary note of August 16th 1938 he stressed that the dramas must be seen together with the didactic plays. Though each play may be understood in isolation, Brecht's aesthetic aims can only be viewed properly in his complete works. With his didactic plays Brecht demonstrated that in a period in which rational tendencies are not valued, the most rational form has the greatest emotional effect; in the same way, at certain times the emphatically social stamp of the figures can make the individual most obvious.

To retain Brecht's terminology, this can only astound those who have a completely conventional picture of the individual. Brecht's efforts in this connection must be viewed in the field of tension between the Puntila and Galileo presentations on one hand, and the demonstration type on the other. But both types of presentation are not simply opposing variations of one and the same problem, they also meet in their intended statement. One type of figure produces, through challenging the public, the same reaction as the other, which makes its statement directly. In his diaries Brecht repeatedly stated that he saw the real step forward in art in the Fatzer type, the "planetary demonstration", rather than the "too opportunist" Galileo figure. For him this was the most valuable contribution he made to the arsenal of new artistic means and artistic experiments. It is only curious that Brecht's actual works did not proceed in the direction of the *Fatzer* fragment.

What is important is that Brecht's contribution to the problem of individuality should not be understood on the basis of the figure-type and also not on the basis of Brecht as a writer on "social" themes. In fact Brecht's efforts should be seen in the framework of the whole wide field which he marked out for himself. Between the two solutions mentioned here there is a wide field which has, by a long mark, not yet been measured. However, the selection of one or the other of these possibilities in order to implement aesthetically the dialectic of the individual and the social is not simply a subjective act of decision on the part of the individual writer. The method in which the problem of individuality is poetically expressed also depends upon the extent to which the social factor is reflected in the consciousness of the individual. The poetical presentation of individuality depends more than anything on the degree of social understanding. This is independent of whether the urgent and important problems confronting society are more or less easily understood in their deepest relations.

Brecht broached a number of philosophical problems in the theoretical and practical work of mastering the dialectic of the individual and society, and these form an important part of the contribution made by Brecht the social theoretician. This should not, however, lead us to forget that this work was also undertaken in order to ensure that the audience was amused and pleased by what he saw in the theatre. Recently both Manfred Wekwerth and Benno Besson, from different angles, have pointed out that the purpose of theatre is to entertain the audience. The sense of a theatrical performance must also appeal to the senses. Brecht brought science into the theatre, not to make it "scientific" but in order to provide new theatrical pleasures for man, who is using science to change society. To be progressive, the theatre must reinforce the old pleasures with new ones. One of the main tasks of Brecht's theatre is to make the audience receptive to new pleasures and better entertainment. Theatre must not come to a halt when faced with the complicated process of the new social developments, and withdraw into the category of the unchangeable. The theatre, if it uses its own specific means, is capable of showing complicated processes in our new reality. Brecht did not want a philosophical theatre, but a theatre in which the philosopher of our advanced society can enjoy himself.

"Art," Brecht wrote, "which adds nothing to the experience of the public, which leaves it as it found it, which wants to do no more than flatter rude instincts and confirm un-ripe or over-ripe opinions — such art is worth nothing. So-called pure entertainment just produces a hangover. There is just as little value in an art which has no purpose but to educate, and thinks to do this by flagellation, abandoning all the varied methods available to the arts; this will not educate the public, but simply bore it. The public have a right to be entertained. This helps to reproduce working strength, but it must not do only this. And the artists have a right to be allowed to entertain."

Through his works Brecht wished to join the ranks of those who aim at helping humanity, easing its existence. He regarded the purport of his work as the illumination of the means of mastering human fate. His work has attained lasting value just because of his efforts to give the people of his day useful books and useful and entertaining theatre. Brecht has become a classic whose works do not aim at making what has been found into something final. His aim was to grasp what is lasting in change.

Brecht has thus become a classic of the literature which aims at great changes in society in the sense of socialism. For our endeavours, now and in the future, his works should be consulted ever and again. To take new paths means to pose new questions to his works.

Sources

JOHANNES R. BECHER, Summer Lament, from *Als namenloses Lied*, 1965.

WALTER BENJAMIN, From the Brecht Commentary, from *Versuche über Brecht*, 1960.

RUTH BERLAU, My First Collaboration with Brecht, from *Neues Deutschland*, 13. 8. 1960.

BERTOLT BRECHT THE DIRECTOR from *Theaterarbeit*, 1952.

ARNOLT BRONNEN, Brecht Directs, from *Tage mit Bertolt Brecht*, 1960.

PAUL DESSAU, How *Lucullus* Came About (written for this volume).

HANNS EISLER, Bertolt Brecht and Music, from *Sinn und Form*, 2. *Brecht-Sonderheft*, 1957.

KONSTANTIN FEDIN, Bertolt Brecht, from *Dichter, Kunst, Zeit*, 1959.

LION FEUCHTWANGER, Bertolt Brecht Presented to the British, from *Die Weltbühne*, 4. 9. 1928.

MAX FRISCH, Diary, 1948, from *Tagebuch 1946–49*, 1950.

BERNARD GUILLEMIN, On What Are You Working? A Talk with Bert Brecht, from *Die Literarische Welt*, 30. 7. 1926.

ELISABETH HAUPTMANN, Notes on Brecht's Work in 1926, from *Sinn und Form*, 2. *Brecht-Sonderheft*, 1957.

WIELAND HERZFELDE, On Bertolt Brecht, from *Neue Deutsche Literatur*, October 1956.

ANGELIKA HURWICZ, Brecht's Work with Actors, from *Sonntag*, 6. 11. 1955.

HERBERT JHERING, Bert Brecht the Dramatist, from *Von Reinhardt bis Brecht*, Vol. I, 1958.

GÜNTER KUNERT, Memories of Bertolt B., from *Kramen in Fächern*, 1968.

LOTTE LENYA-WEILL, Threepenny Opera, from *Bertolt Brechts Dreigroschenbuch*, 1960.

WERNER MITTENZWEI, Brecht 1973 – Speech on his 75th Birthday, from *Sonntag*, August 1973.

HANNS OTTO MÜNSTERER, Recollections of Brecht in 1919 in Augsburg, from *Panorama*, August 1959.

CASPAR NEHER, In Memory of My Friend, from *Sinn und Form*, 2. *Brecht-Sonderheft*, 1957.

VLADIMIR POZNER, bb, from *Sinn und Form*, 2. *Brecht-Sonderheft*, 1957.

BERNHARD REICH, Recollections of Brecht as a Young Man, from *Sinn und Form*, 2. *Brecht-Sonderheft*, 1957.

PAUL RILLA, Brecht from 1918 to 1950, from *Essays*, 1955.

KÄTHE RÜLICKE-WEILER, "Since then the World has Hope", from *Neue Deutsche Literatur*, February 1968.

MAX SCHROEDER, Brecht's Stage Style, from *Von hier und heute aus*, 1957.

ERNST SCHUMACHER, He Will Remain, from *Neue Deutsche Literatur*, October 1956.

ANNA SEGHERS, Brecht, from *Sinn und Form*, 2. *Brecht-Sonderheft*, 1957.

STAGE TECHNICIANS RELATE, from *Sinn und Form*, 2. *Brecht-Sonderheft*, 1957.

ERWIN STRITTMATTER, Journeyman Years with Brecht, from *Wochenpost*, 9. 8. 1958.

SERGEI TRETYAKOV, Bert Brecht, from *Das internationale Theater* (Moscow), No. 3/4, 1934.

BERTHOLD VIERTEL, Brecht, Robbed of Citizenship, from *Die neue Weltbühne* (Paris), 3. 2. 1938.

GÜNTER WEISENBORN, Zurich Diary, from *Sinn und Form*, 2. *Brecht-Sonderheft*, 1957.

MANFRED WEKWERTH, Discovering an Aesthetic Category, from *Sinn und Form*, 2. *Brecht-Sonderheft*, 1957.

ARNOLD ZWEIG, Brecht Summary, from *Neue deutsche Blätter* (Prague), December 1934.